Notes Taken At The Time

A collection of true stories from the beat

Illustrations by PC John Whittaker of Cheshire

Police Review Publishing Company,
14 St. Cross Street, London EC1N 8FE

ISBN 0 85164 005 2

Computerset by Promenade Graphics Limited, Cheltenham and printed by Page Bros. (Norwich) Limited

Authors' royalties will be given to The Police Pensioners' Housing Association

The Police Pensioners' Housing Association has been formed to provide accommodation for pensioners or their widows who are spending their declining years in substandard housing, perhaps deprived of all contact with former colleagues. Their number is not great, but the need is real, and it is hoped that everyone who respects the traditions of the police service in this country, will help those retired officers who helped to consolidate that tradition.

CONTENTS

FOREWORD

by **Sir Robert Mark, GBE, QPM,** former Commissioner of the Metropolitan Police

Some years ago a distinguished actress, when offering thanks for the conferment of an honorary degree, remarked that of all the countless occasions on which she had spoken in public this was the first on which she had used words not written by others. Her speech was short, intelligent and witty. It gave the large audience a brief insight of her as a person rather than an actress.

I reflected then that policemen are in much the same position. The public impression of them is shaped by the routine events and procedures of their public appearances, or by the newspaper, the television screen or the crime novel. Very few people even consider the police as human beings with some of the virtues, failings and talents common to all. Perhaps even more than the possible advantages of what is called 'community policing'—whatever that means—is that the public should understand better that the police really are part of the community and not a class apart.

The stories in this book will help to achieve that end. They are not masterpieces of literacy. They do not deal with the usual police headline topics: murder, mayhem and so on. But they are unpretentious, enjoyable and they do reveal the personalities behind the uniform—or the plain clothes. And since I happen to believe that the police are one of the most admirable and, in particular, best motivated of our public services and organisations, I think revelation of this unpretentious kind can do nothing but good.

Robert Mark
7th June, 1983

1 The Life and Death of a Canine Academy Drop-out

by Stanley Millward

One Thursday in January 1981, I set off from home for the Lancashire County Constabulary Police Dog Training School. My mission was to take on a young police dog who had quite simply failed his course. Very sensibly he was gun shy—guns terrified him.

I had never seen him, but I knew he was there. I would have taken him whether he was handsome, plain or ugly—but he was in fact a beautiful German Sheepdog who came loping, into the sergeant's office.

His most noticeable feature for me was his sheer beauty—his next noticeable feature was that he had one ear up and one ear almost down—hiding, I was later to discover, a deep-seated pain.

The dog's name was Zep. From that moment he became my dog, and he was to remain so until his death at 10am on Saturday, December 19, 1981, but that day is the end of my story, so let us return to the beginning.

Zep and I left for home, where he was to join my old Alsatian, Sheba, a fit 15-year-old; Tara, my overweight black Labrador bitch and Toby, my cross-bred Terrier—a scruff of the dog world.

Zep was then 14 months old. He had started his professional career in the prison service at Durham. Then the Lancashire Constabulary, my old force, took over his training. I never knew or asked why they did, but evidently, for all their expertise, he wasn't going to make it and that's where I and my family came in; both humans and animals gave him a permanent and very loving home.

I remember thinking on my way home that he and I were both in our own ways products of the police service, both of us had in some ways failed, and both perhaps bore deep-seated scars. I suspected his may have been the result of being too near the discharge of a shotgun, and mine—what had caused mine?

After 25 years in the CID, I was commander of the District Task Force. The deputy of the force with which we amalgamated in 1974 had definite views on task forces.

'Oh yes,' said the deputy, 'I know task forces, they are just body snatchers.' The discharge was too near *my* ear. I reacted arrogantly and without discretion (I have been accused of both failings). 'The police force and the public,' I said, 'will be the worse off if you don't have task forces.'

For some reason I was posted back to a division, to take over from a detective chief inspector. I had already had three county divisions as detective inspector and detective chief inspector and had been a district superintendent since '67. Some people even said I was a good one.

Well, the new force didn't get a task force, I wasn't called in for interview for detective chief superintendent, and because of well wishers and my own arrogance, got a city division, Longsight, instead.

But that is all a long time ago; the deputy chief went on to higher things and GMP, much later, got a type of task force.

It was recently engaged in the Moss Side and, I believe, the Toxteth riots.

Fancy thinking all that, just because of a failed police dog? Let us return to Zep. In spite of frequent veterinary attention his ear never did completely cease troubling him, but after each visit to the vet it would stand beautifully to complement the other, but gradually the pain would return.

The seasons passed, and throughout it all we were very close. Sheba, the old Alsatian, for whom an early death had been forecast and whose place in the animal hierarchy Zep had been intended to take, grew more active, obviously relishing the ardent, though platonic, attentions of her intended replacement.

Perhaps by coincidence two things happened on the night of December 10. One was the sub-zero temperature and the other was that Zep went off his food. He had always eaten well, but he was much, much too thin.

The veterinary surgeon, a young Scottish girl, didn't seem to know what was wrong, but she said, 'Oh dear'. It was a very human, though perhaps unprofessional, remark but she was, I thought, a woman first and a vet second.

A subsequent vist to her resulted in much the same

treatment—the inevitable needle—but this time Zep couldn't jump on to the table, and I had to lift him on.

He had eaten hardly anything and my wife and I fed him liquid glucose by way of bottle and teat. He accepted it with difficulty but reproached us, I think, for doing what we had to do.

On the morning of Saturday, December 19, he gently and without, I believe, much pain, died in our living room. The morning was brightly sunny and I disturbed the pure white snow in the paddock to dig a grave, with clean straw on the bottom.

A neighbour walked past exercising his dog and called out 'Digging for gold?". 'No,' I replied, 'just burying some'.

Stanley Millward, *58, is a retired Detective Superintendent. He served with Greater Manchester Police for 28½ years.*

2 Damsel in Distress

by Andrew Chinn

I'm on panda working nights with Roger and get this call at 3am—'Ombersley Road, woman locked out of flat'. Off we go in our Mini. It's this house converted into flats and she's on the doorstep, shivering in lacy lingerie!

'Sorry. I couldn't sleep. I got up to make a cup of tea, opened the door to put the milk bottles out and it shut behind me.'

Says Roger: 'There's an easy solution to this. Wake the old man.' She looks apologetic, saying, 'He's the heaviest sleeper in the world.'

We decide to try anyway. The flat's on the first floor and upstairs we go. I try knocking, then Roger, then our damsel. Nothing. We try it a bit louder, then with truncheons and empty milk bottles. No reply except the bloke opposite comes out in his 'jim-jams' and threatens to call the police, sees us and hastily disappears.

This is no good. Then she tells us the old man is languishing in the bedroom at the back of the house, and there's no access except through the downstairs flat. Down we go, and knock on the door. No reply.

Then we give it fists and boots. Then a woman living opposite comes out and threatens to call the police. Still no reply. Back up the stairs and we try our own house keys in madam's lock. Then the panda keys, then Roger tries a bit of wire he's got.

Hopeless! So we all try the flat downstairs again. Eventually we hear shuffling and mumbling—'Who's there, go away or I'll call the police.'

It then takes us ages to convince this girl who we are (incidentally, she has a terrible bout of 'flu). She lets us through to the rear, leaps back into bed and pulls the covers up to her chin.

At the back of the building, it's so dark it could be a black hole. We slip, and crash into a bike by some dustbins. Lights come on all over the neighbourhood. We see people peering

"ER... IS YOUR HUSBAND
A BIG BLOKE ?"

through windows clutching old boots and pots of water, and hearing repeated mutterings of 'Bloody cats'.

The light's on in the bedroom above and we throw pebbles at the window. No response. Then Roger climbs on top of the coal shed and just can't reach the window, even by holding his truncheon at arm's length.

Down he comes—the quick way! On to those bins again. He really has a natural ability for noise. Oh God! This is awful!

'I know,' she says. 'Use the line prop and tap on the window.' So I do, several times, and crack one of the panes. But still sleeping beauty doesn't wake. I let the line prop fall and it goes crashing and bouncing across the yard. This is getting worse . . .

Police training then comes into play—Roger goes up the drainpipe to the outhouse roof hoping to see into the bedroom. He gets stuck and we have to rescue him.

We stand defeated. 'My dad's got a ladder,' she says. Great! Good idea! Where's your dad live? Only half a mile away . . .

Well now we're desperate and this sounds good. Off we go, Roger recovering from vertigo, her in the back shivering in her negligee, and me giggling in the front.

We arrive at 'dad's house'. They're related—it takes 15 minutes to wake him. We bang and kick the door, throw pebbles at the window and swear a good deal. The whole family wakes and comes to various windows, then half the street.

'What's our Christine doing with you?' We explain. The news spreads like wildfire and is accepted with jubilation. Cups of tea appear and a carnival atmosphere prevails.

The ladder has to be Victorian—it weighs a ton. It's a good 20 ft and won't quite fit in the panda, I, as junior man, am elected to carry it to the flat. It's 3.30 am and me in full uniform strolling along with this enormous ladder on my shoulder. I arrive panting.

Next to get the ladder to the back of the house. We wake the girl again and, between the three of us and shouted directions of the 'flu sufferer from her sick bed, we take the ladder through the downstairs flat. With us come the kitchen curtains and several knick-knacks off the mantelpiece.

The moment arrives, the ladder is set up at the bedroom window. We toss up for the glory of waking the old man. Roger wins and up the ladder he goes to open the window and wake the sleeping wonder.

At the top he looks down in despair. 'It's nailed down.' 'Oh yes,' she agrees, 'He did that last Easter, it rattled. Sorry. Really.'

We wrestle the ladder back through the flat and past the girl, who by now has the covers completely over her head.

Frontal assault next. The kitchen window next. Ladder up, and Roger streaks up like a ferret. Incredible, the window opens and in he goes. We see the soles of his boots just before he disappears and cries out in anguish as he dives into the washing boiler.

This is the moment of truth. I look at my scantily-clad companion and together we start towards the front door.

Well. You'll never believe this, but my pal Roger is so exultant at getting into the flat, he doesn't wake up our hostage (planning for the three of us to do it together). Instead, he goes through the kitchen, the hall, and out through the door.

Standing at the top of the stairs he calls down, 'I'm in'. Then . . . 'CLUNK'. The door closes smoothly behind him.

I see a desperate panic in his eyes as he streaks past, out into the garden, up the ladder, and into the flat again.

He grandly opens the door. A pot of tea is made and some 20 minutes later, 'She' puts her cup down and runs into the bedroom. 'I forgot him,' she shrieks. We exchange looks. Yes, we did too, missus.

She comes back, looking relieved. 'He's still asleep and on earlies today, I'm sure he'd like to meet you. *In a couple of minutes he'll be getting up with the alarm*. Perhaps you'd like to . . . '

That's all we heard, Roger was already furiously starting the panda. I looked back and chanced to see the happy pair waving from the kitchen window. Some people!

Andrew Chinn *is a PC in the Traffic Department in West Mercia Constabulary. He is 27 and has 7½ years' service. He is married to Jane and has a daughter, Hayley, aged two.*

3 The Pendleton Rodeo

by Bill Kerr

Re-development had not yet affected the narrow terraced streets and decaying factories of Pendleton in the late Sixties. It's populace, locally called 'Pengys', rarely strayed over the district's boundaries.

Sgt W. and I, in a sparkling new Morris Minor panda, were patrolling the area during a Sunday afternoon in late summer. A radio message directed us to the abbatoir of Manchester Meats, from where a cow had escaped.

Along Broughton Road we sighted our quarry, an obviously agitated Friesian cow being pursued by a posse of red-faced Pengys only recently dismissed from local public houses. The demented cow hurtled past us, bucking and kicking, towards Littleton Road and, she hoped, freedom.

Sgt W. leaned from the car window shouting at the pursuers to leave the creature alone, but the more he shouted the more intrigued bystanders joined in the chase.

When it arrived at Littleton Road the posse was more than 100 strong. Pengys were hanging from the windows of speeding cars brandishing lassoes made from washing lines, and small boys pedalled frantically behind them.

We were joined by the pride of the senior officers' fleet, a new, bright-blue Mini saloon, bearing Insp F., sucking on his cigar.

Between two council houses was a narrow footpath leading to Pendleton's green belt, a handkerchief-sized corner of litter-strewn ground. Here the cow was trapped, as Insp F., in a masterly display of initiative, parked the Mini and effectively blocked the footpath. We began to break up the throng.

The Chief Superintendent, on weekend duty, felt compelled to attend an incident which by now had gathered considerable momentum. Anyway, the prospect of a rodeo in Pendleton was not to be missed. Insp F., with a smart salute, was just directing the Chief Super's attention to where the cow was trapped when, with a tremendous, anguished echoing bellow the animal thundered along the entry, watched by two bemused, open-mouthed senior ranks, and hurtled straight on to the new car and over the bonnet and roof. Then she was off again, on her way towards the Littleton Road playing fields, bordered by the River Irwell.

The Pendleton Cowboys were again in pursuit. In an attempt to quell hysteria, I raced to the head of the chasing mob and got there in time to see an elderly woman leaving her front gate to see what the noise was about. Her arrival coincided with that of the cow and she was left trampled and unconscious in the gutter. I stayed with her until an ambulance arrived. Meanwhile, the evergrowing posse surged ahead.

Our cow was now confined, in her confusion, on the playing fields. She was flanked by a line of policemen keeping back a crowd reaching football match proportions.

The driver who had been delivering the beast to the abbatoir was sent for, with his vehicle, to collect his charge, which was now snorting and pawing the ground.

Two young boys appeared over the river bank 400 yards distant, walking inquisitively towards the assembled crowd. Shouts from the crowd failed to warn them, but obviously alerted the cow.

Young PC W., aware of the imminent danger to the boys, detached himself from the police ranks and proceeded cautiously across the field waving his arms in the hope of attracting their attention. The boys didn't see him. He ventured even further.

The cow had clearly waited for him to pass the point of no return before lowering her head and charging. With great presence of mind PC W., attempted to hide behind the only available static object—a goalpost.

The crowd were cheering wildly, some encouraging the officer, and many the cow—but not for long. The cow's head connected with goalpost at full speed. The post snapped and PC W., travelled through the air in a perfect arc, still clutching the broken timber. He landed in the goalmouth, only to suffer further indignity of a thorough trampling by 10 cwt of pie-filling-to-be.

The injured were later released from hospital and the cow safely loaded and pointed in the direction of the abbatoir. An unfortunate finale for the provider of Pendleton's only rodeo.

Bill Kerr *is an Inspector in Greater Manchester Police. He is 37 and has had 17 years' service. He is married with three sons.*

4 A Lesson in Protest

by John Chapman

In the early '70s, before the IRA's activities created the need for a full-time Special Branch, the odd demonstration was farmed out in my division to a senior-citizen detective sergeant, who was less active in the day-to-day operations of catching thieves—me.

Thus it was that I was told that an organisation known as the Anti-Apartheid League was going to demonstrate at a local sports ground, where a selected white South African cricket team sponsored by a South African millionaire was to play the county team. The plan of campaign was that a dozen uniformed Bobbies would be hidden in a van near the ground, while I, with my muscle support, big Taff, would observe and report back by that then marvel of communication, the personal radio. That was it. No more forward planning than that.

I made some enquiries to find out what was the Anti-Apartheid League. No one had heard of it, so it was with some confidence that Taff and I attended the ground on the day. It was a lovely summer day, with half a dozen people exercising their dogs on various parts of the pitch and the playing area.

I tested my PR. 'Oscar One to Control. Are you receiving? Over.'

'Yea. Got you clear, John,' was the reply. Always sticklers for procedure, that lot.

Taff and I took up a position in the beer tent. After about an hour's play there were still no more than 50 people strung out around the boundary, plus a couple of the exercising dogs, who were showing more signs of life than the spectators.

As we were on our fourth pint, and it was likely to be a long day, I pulled rank on the reluctant Taff and we went for a stroll. For no other reason than that we had walked a full 200 yards, we stopped behind a long wooden seat on which were grouped about six nice kids. They had to be nice because at the time they were discussing the Spurs team and its prospects in the coming season.

I must admit that I did notice one of them was wearing an Automobile Association badge and it did strike me that the colours were unusual. Still, even in those days, youngsters wore badges just for the sake of it. Such was my character assessment of that little group. Wrong again.

Just when Taffy was inquiring when we were going to get back to the tent, the youngsters were on their feet and running towards the wicket area, with others joining them from different parts of the ground. Taffy rushed off after the group to take the one nearest the wicket, while I followed on and managed to catch the one furthest from it. As I touched him on the shoulder to inquire what it was all about, he threw himself to the ground, hands on top of his head, face into the grass.

Bloody Hell, I thought, kneeling down and putting my knee on the prone figure, just in case. Just in case of what? I dunno.

I operated my PR. 'Oscar One to Control. Are you receiving?' Nothing. 'Oscar One to Control. Are you receiving?' Again nothing.

'Oscar One to Control. Are you receiving me?' By now I was several octaves higher than on the first call.

'What's the matter, John?' At last!

'Get out here quick. There's a crowd of bloody idiots on the pitch.'

'I'm not an idiot,' said an indignant voice from under my right knee.

'Shut up. I'm not speaking to you,' I told him.

After what seemed a life time, the Chief Inspector led his 12 men in double time formation from the pavilion and through the roped-off batsmen's entry to the pitch. It looked more like a scene from *The Pirates of Penzance*.

Meanwhile, big Taff, with the help of the stray dogs, had herded the protesters together and shepherded them in my direction. The leader, a well-spoken young man, identified himself. Our conversation went something like this:

Me: Is this your first demo?

Him: I'm afraid it is.

'I thought it was. You don't know the rules. In future, you contact the senior security branch officer at the scene; tell him what you intend to do. He will arrange for you to make your point and then you get escorted away. You will have done your bit; we will have done ours. Understand?'

'Oh yes. I'm frightfully sorry. I wasn't aware of what was required.'

'That's all right this time, but what are you going to do now? I've got these uniform chaps on overtime and I don't want them hanging about for nothing if that was it.'

'We were going to get a lot of support from a London contingent on scooters, but they haven't materialised. We'll call it a day.'

'Now be fair. I don't want to send the police away and then have a repetition. You will all be escorted from the ground, and will that be the end?'

'Definitely! At five bob a go we can't afford to come back inside again.'

'Well, what's your next move?'

'We will continue to protest against this team at their next match in Oxford.'

Formal shaking of hands all round and end of story. Well, not quite . . .

I phoned my counterpart at Oxford and gave him the background and information I had gathered.

'What do you think of the strength of it?' he said.

'To be fair,' I replied, 'their actions were nothing more than pricks of annoyance.'

Two days later he phoned me and, in a very uptight voice, said: 'Those pricks of annoyance have just dug up the bloody pitch!'

That leader certainly learned the rules fast.

John Chapman, *60, retired from Essex Police as a Detective Sergeant, after 29 years' service. He has two married sons, and four grandchildren.*

5 Book the Duke

by John Pearson

It was the Superintendent on the phone. 'How good is your French?' he asked. 'I'm thinking of recommending you for a job in Paris.' I assured him it was reasonable, although the moment I put the phone down I began to have doubts. Was I fluent enough to work in France?

For several weeks I waited for the call. Then, late one Thursday afternoon, it came 'Go to London Airport, Saturday. Catch the 12 noon plane to Orly with Tony Paddy and you will be met by British embassy officials at the airport. Why you are going and for what purpose, I just don't know,' said my Super, anticipating an odd question or two.

After some minor problems, including the temporary loss of Tony's hat, we cleared the plane and customs at Orly. There was no one who looked remotely like a British embassy official anywhere in the reception area. After we had made some fruitless inquiries, we were approached by a taxi driver and a rather chic mademoiselle who, having checked off our names, invited us to follow her.

By now Tony Paddy and myself were allowing our imaginations to run amok. Had the French connection been made? Where were they taking us?

Fortunately, the young lady spoke reasonable English. 'My boss is Eddie Barclay,' she said, 'the French millionaire, and you are now being taken to your hotel. I will call for you at 10 pm to take you along to the party.' She said she knew nothing about any British embassy officials, so we didn't pursue the subject.

We had quite a hectic half day in Paris and then returned to our hotel for a rest in the evening. Unfortunately, our charming French friend rang to say she was having trouble with her party dress—a woman's privilege—so a taxi would take us directly to the party.

Our driver first thought we were in fancy dress as we left for the Pavilion on the other side of Paris. When he realised we

"AND I SUPPOSE YOU'RE SIR ROBERT MARK."
GLC

were the real McCoy—genuine English Bobbies in uniform—he could not believe it. It did our nerves no good at all the way he sped along, looking over his shoulder and chattering away.

We arrived in one piece at the Pavilion to a scene of swinging London. There were red buses, black cabs, fireworks and Union Jacks (many run upside down!) outside. There was even artificial fog creeping up to the entrance. Inside were English bands, good English food and drink and a roaring party in progress. It seemed we were there to add a further touch of authenticity.

Among the Cavaliers, Roundheads, boy scouts, smart city gents and even Frenchmen disguised as British PCs, were the Belles of St. Trinian's, who were certainly having a ball. One of them, taller than the rest, was really kicking up a shindig.

During the height of the exciting and inciting rock and roll performance one of them broke off and sidled up to Tony Paddy and myself. The St. Trinian's garb didn't fool us one little bit, for this was obviously a lady of some repute.

In a sexy French accent she said: 'My husband is really creating quite a disturbance.' She identified him as the tallest one in the group. 'I can tell you are real English Bobbies. Would you please arrest him and throw him out. Just for fun.'

Tony Paddy and I looked at each other, smiled graciously at the lovely lady, and got to work. Then, we took the long lanky St. Trinian's girl by each arm and, amid some protest from our captive, led her away from her gyrating friends.

A few moments later an unidentified English voice at my elbow made a stunning observation: 'My word! You've just arrested and thrown out the Duke of Bedford, you know.'

So we had. The gracious lady was the Duchess and, yes, this tall, distinguished-looking person who we had laid our hands on was, without doubt, her husband, the Duke. And the other Belles included Twiggy and Mary Quant.

For a moment we were rather embarrassed—to say the least. But the Duke soon put us at our ease by identifying himself and inviting us to join him and his party.

It was the first time I have been involved in the 'arrest' of a real Duke, even if it was on foreign soil and a refused charge. Will it be the last? Anyone seen Lord Lucan?

John Pearson *is an Inspector in Thames Valley Police. He is 46, has 25 years' service and is married with two sons and one daughter.*

6 Curly Harry

by Jay Field

He was called 'Curly' because of his bald pate; my first encounter with him was on a cold morning in November 1965, when I was on early shift in the town centre of Evesham. And I smelt him before I saw him.

He came shuffling down Bridge Street, a tubby old man dressed in a filthy grey overcoat which reached to his ankles, a battered old cloth cap and a pair of shoe uppers (the soles had long since gone and had been replaced by cardboard). He carried a plastic bag with his worldly possessions.

If one could have seen smells, his would have been a mile high. The people on the footpath were giving him a wide berth but I could see he was making a bee-line for me and was unable to get away.

I held my breath as he came nearer. Giving me a toothless grin he said: 'Hello, duck, can you give me a couple of pence for a cuppa? I'm ever so cold.'

Rising to my full 5ft 6in I stuck out my chest importantly and intoned the terms of the Vagrancy Act etc.

His grin faded and he said: 'You're all the same you coppers. I thought you'd be different. I don't do no 'arm, I just like to live differently.'

He turned away and suddenly all my authority left me. I stopped him, gave him a two shilling piece and told him to go and get warm. The tears of gratitude in his eyes were enough thanks for me.

So, I was stuck with a tramp for a friend. Whenever I was on duty, Curly would be around with a toothless happy grin and a merry wave and few words of 'wisdom' for me.

I realised that I knew virtually nothing of this man. We exchanged pleasantries, we put up with him because he was the local character and didn't cause any trouble, but what was he really like? What had made him live a life of a tramp and recluse?

I took time to talk to him and he told me his real name was Arthur Smythe and he came from Leicestershire. He had

HEY UP LOVE.
DO YER FANCY
A TRAMP IN
THE PARK

decided many years ago to walk the countryside because he didn't know what to do with all the money he had inherited, and he didn't want to give it away!

(It transpired later that he had a considerable sum which eventually went to a sister in Canada.)

He hadn't realised that it was so difficult to live without money. He had numerous stories to tell about life on the road and he had found a fascinated listener.

He had no intention of going back to the old life because he hadn't long to live. When I asked him how he knew this, he said he had had a dream of dying in a wooded area.

I arranged for him to be de-loused at regular intervals in the local centre, and he looked unrecognisable when he came out wearing second-hand clothes supplied by the local WRVS.

The only thing I couldn't get him was money, and even though he did have lots tucked away somewhere he still resorted to begging when my back was turned.

One day we had a lady rush into the station saying that a dirty old man had accosted her two small daughters and made them scream. She was convinced that he had indecently assaulted them.

Myself and a colleague went on a search for this 'dirty old man' and found Curly sitting on a park bench chewing on a ham sandwich that he had extricated from a litter bin. The little girls were sitting on the bench quite happily with him and he was telling them stories.

They hadn't been assaulted in any way. Mum just didn't like the look of him. Curly said the girls reminded him of his sister and he had felt lonely.

He had become quite a celebrity in town. Everyone knew Curly, even though few stopped to talk to him. The shopkeepers began leaving titbits out for him and he was given old clothing. Even though the food was stale, Curly ate it with relish. Never had he been so well looked after.

Christmas time drew near and everyone in the town was full of bustle making arrangements—and in amongst us all was Curly still walking the streets.

How he kept warm is a mystery. He slept in a tent of twigs and branches in a copse just out of town. He refused to go into a home.

I met him one morning just before Christmas and he gave me a small packet, untidily wrapped in old newspaper. He said: 'This is for you, it was my mother's and I want you to have it. You have been kind to me and I appreciate it. Happy Christmas.'

With that he walked away and I undid the parcel. In it was a small lace handkerchief and a packet of mints. I still have that handkerchief.

Two days later, on Christmas day, we were called to a small copse on the Birmingham Road and there, lying on some leaves and covered with sacking, was Curly Harry. He had been dead for about 10 hours. His dream had come true. He was buried in a pauper's grave in the local cemetery. He had one mourner—me.

Underneath the dirt, Curly was a very special human being with much compassion for his fellow men. It's a pity we couldn't have treated him the same. He left me a lesson I won't easily forget.

Jay Field *is a Sergeant in West Mercia Police. She is 40 years old, has 20 years' service, and is single.*

7 A Symmetrical Accident

by Sean Hollands

I learned two lessons at Ashford, my first posting after training school.

First, young probationers are unwise to book the superintendent's bank manager for parking in the no-waiting area outside his own bank on a pay day.

Second, the sergeant will express no interest or sympathy whatsoever for the injuries one sustains in the middle of a foggy night by falling through the rotten flap of a cellar owned by the chairman of the bench, especially when one's night-duty colleague is simultaneously covering himself with glory by poaching on your beat to notch up the first night arrest for over a year. He caught his burglar red-handed in a wholesale tobacconist's not 50 yards from the cellar flap in question.

My transfer to Maidstone after a year must have been a blessed relief to the metropolis of Ashford. I was determined to do better at my new station but the first few minutes of one of my first late-turn shifts showed it wasn't going to be easy.

It had been a wet day, but as I left the station for the High Street beat I noticed the rain had stopped and the sun had come out. Gabriels Hill was then a steep, narrow, one-way street, which carried a heavy flow of downhill traffic. Vehicles were allowed to park on their offside only at the foot of the hill, where the road levelled off.

The driver of a small van was vainly trying to pull away from the kerb into the nonstop flow of traffic. He was no doubt pleased to have his problem solved by this efficient young policeman who, in no time, had successfully and carefully stopped a Land-Rover coming down the hill (looking back I wish I had never seen this little man with his problem). Having satisfied myself that the Land-Rover had stopped, I turned my back on it to wave out the van driver. Too late. He must have been in a hurry, for he was well out of sight.

As I turned back to wave on the Land-Rover, with left arm

raised in the approved signal, a riveting sight met my eyes. The Land-Rover passenger had decided to make the most of this temporary hold-up to alight.

He was swinging open the nearside door, an action unremarkable in itself. The interesting thing was the course being taken by a head-down, bottom-up cyclist, doing all of 30 mph down the nearside of the Land-Rover.

As we all know, cycle brakes are next to useless in the wet. But this was of no concern to the rider, whose nose was so close to the mudguard that he couldn't possibly have noticed the presence of the Law holding up the traffic, let alone the stationary Land-Rover and its rapidly opening nearside door.

Although he did not see the need for a bit of swift braking, he did avoid the awful prospect of 'failing to conform to the signal of a police officer engaged for the time being in the regulation, etc' by the simple expedient of running head first into the now fully open door.

The most surprised party must have been the Land-Rover passenger, as the door was snatched from his grasp and flung back against the front wing. The most petrified, without a doubt, was me—mainly at the prospect of having to perform my first live first aid.

The most blasé was the cyclist. He had had no idea of the misfortune about to befall him, nor of the misfortune that already had. He was sitting bolt upright on the footpath, leaning against the wall of a pub, looking for all the world like a tramp waiting for opening time. He had no worries at all, for he was unconscious with a broken leg.

My left arm was still raised in frozen immobility . . .

The only parts of me that functioned were my eyes, following the progress of a rather bent and riderless cycle as it careered down the footpath, weaving among some pedestrians until it disappeared through the front door of Radio Rentals. This swift removal from the scene of one of the participating vehicles would have been quite satisfying had the shop door been open at the time.

As the crash of shattering plate glass subsided, the rising tones of a hysterical shop assistant did nothing to help my left arm relax.

Any attempt to restore normal bodily functions was doomed to failure. The hideous screech of tortured tyres dragged my reluctant eyes away from the shattered door to a two-ton lorry coming down the hill behind the Land-Rover.

Its driver had not woken up to the fact that the thunderous progress of traffic down Maidstone's steepest hill had been halted until it was a wee bit too late. Still, at least he had the decency not to inflict a second hammering on the Land-Rover, and mounted the crowded offside footpath.

The front offside wing, fortunately made of flexible rubber, swept a 12-year-old girl off her feet, and her hand out of that of her mother, walking beside her. It then crashed through the window of Beale's baby shop, neatly depositing the girl, complete with broken leg, on to an inflatable bed, on display in the window. (The ambulance crew left her on this giving her the softest ride to hospital any casualty could ever have wished for.)

The lorry effectively blocked access to the shop and to the injured girl, with the result that mother's hysterics were soon rivalling those of the assistant on the other side of the road.

My left arm was still raised . . .

The rising pandemonium eventually brought me to my senses and I got my arm down. After a quick inspection of the still unconscious cyclist, I found the only way to reach the girl on the bed was through the neighbouring funeral parlour, which had a connecting door to the baby shop.

It struck me that things could not have been a lot worse. Her flight path could have taken her through the other window, straight into a waiting coffin. I thought it unwise to mention this when trying to calm mother down.

Later, back at the station, I found my inspector was not a happy man and was even less happy when I mentioned the good fortune re the funeral parlour.

But it was his reaction when I pointed out that it was really a very neat and symmetrical accident—one damaged vehicle, one injured person with broken leg, one hysterical woman and one broken shop window on *each* side of the road—that told me it was about time I returned to the beat.

As I left the station yet again for the High Street, I noticed the sun had gone in and it had begun raining again . . .

Sean Hollands *is a PC in Kent County Constabulary. He is 43, has 21½ years' service and is married to Rosemary. He has two daughters, Susan, aged 15, and Victoria, 10. He has recently returned after three years with the Royal Papua New Guinea Constabulary.*

8 The Gasman Calleth

by Peter Evans

It was just after 11 am on my fourth consecutive morning of early turn when the radio directed me to Lancaster Road. I believe the sun was shining, although it did not matter much: my plans for the afternoon were to have 40 winks in the armchair before the children got home from school. For some time now they had been discreetly referring to me as 'The Dosser' because, as I had overheard them explaining to their friends, whenever I sat down I fell asleep and occasionally dribbled on my tie. The joys of shift work.

I was the acting sergeant and had Stan, an enthusiastic young probationer, with me in the car. The controller told us the gasman was having trouble getting into the house of Theopolus Brown to read the meter. Just the sort of job for Stan, I thought. He needs some practice at the art of gentle persuasion.

The gasman was short, stout and wore a faded blue belted raincoat. Under his arm he carried a well-thumbed, hard-backed book. He looked relieved to see us and, as he leant against the gatepost, said: 'All I want to do is read the meter. This is the third time I've been refused entry.' Stan nodded knowledgeably and knocked authoritatively on the front door, which was almost immediately opened by Theopolus, a muscular West Indian, of about 40, wearing a vest and trousers.

'May the gasman read your meter?' asked Stan, going straight to the heart of the matter.

'It doesn't work, officer,' came the reply.

'May we have a look at it? asked Stan. To our surprise Theopolus walked back into the hall and stood looking at the shelf behind the front door where one would have expected to see the meter. There was none there. Instead, the main gas inlet pipe had been connected directly to the household piping by a rubber hose and clips.

"HONESTLY MR BROWN, IT'S THE PRETTIEST AND BEST HANDBAG THAT WE HAVE EVER SEEN."

'Who did that?' I asked indicating the handiwork and looking round to see if anyone was smoking.

'I did,' said Theopolus proudly. 'I couldn't get any gas out of the meter so I removed it.'

'Where is it now?' I inquired apprehensively, not wishing to stay in the house a minute longer than necessary.

'Upstairs,' he grinned. I followed him up to his bedroom. On the dressing table was the meter. All its paint had been scraped off and its bare metal shone like a new pin. On the top, between the inlet and outlet pipes, was tied a short, thick piece of coloured rope.

He hoisted the meter by the rope and we went downstairs. The gasman apparently had a sensitive disposition and a good nose for trouble. As soon as he saw Theopolus appear in the hall beaming broadly and carrying the meter like a handbag he slipped out the front door. We did not see him again that day.

Stan looked a little perplexed. At training school they had taught him about the offence of abstracting electricity, but they had not mentioned diverting gas and turning the meter into an ornament.

'Humour him, Stan,' I muttered 'while I go to the car for the cuffs.' As I walked down the garden path I heard a high-pitched, urgent voice calling my name. Either Stan had had a sudden and severe attack of laryngitis or someone was interfering with his respiratory system.

I found Theopolus had Stan the Communicator pinned to the wall. He had a hand on his throat and, with his left knee, was trying to ruin the young man's marital prospects. 'I ain't going nowhere with you, man,' he chanted, and looked as if he meant it.

The fight that ensued while we waited for help was one-sided, to say the least. Lord Scarman should have been there.

I remember wishing as I was knocked backwards through the kitchen window that I had the stuntman's knack of falling without injury. The sound of Stan's truncheon splitting as he vainly attempted to persuade Theopolus to come quietly will remain with me forever. Fortunately, the arrival of more police officers seemed to have a tranquillising effect on the prospective prisoner.

Early turn can be testing, I reflected, as I dozed off in the chair that afternoon.

Peter Evans *is an Inspector in the Avon and Somerset Constabulary. He is 41 years old, has 13 years' service and is married to Hazel. He has a son, Laurence, 17, and a daughter, Tanya, 14.*

9 The Black Dog

by John Beaumont

At Chantmarle near Dorchester, where I did my initial training, the practicals included exercises known as 'beat incidents' supposed to equip us with the necessary expertise to handle day-to-day policing. Or, perhaps they were intended to warn us of the wild and woolly world we would shortly enter.

One of these beat incidents started as a domestic dispute between two brothers, then introduced more characters to assail the unsuspecting PC until he was trying to deal simultaneously with the original domestic, a Chinaman who spoke no English, an Arab with a handgun, and a man enveloped in a bright yellow sleeping bag claiming to be going to a fancy dress party as a banana.

All good training, we told ourselves, but hardly typical police work.

I am now serving at a rural station where virtually nothing stirs after midnight. Virtually . . .

Panda patrol, one o'clock in the morning. The radio crackles into life: ' . . . make 17, one seven, High Street, two people savaged by dog. Ambulance attending.'

No 17 the High Street is a green grocer's with living quarters above. The family pet is a large black Alsatian called Satan. Tony and I entered the shop and started to climb the stairs to the flat. We broke into a run as we saw blood daubed along the wall and banister rail.

We ignored the room that obviously contained Satan from the scratching, snarling and howling coming from it and stepped into a scene from a Hammer horror film.

In the living room were two girls with blood on their hands, arms and the front of their dresses. An older woman, her clothes soaked with blood, was staggering about screaming. She was holding her arm, which had an enormous gash in it from which blood was still spraying.

The tableau was completed by the son of the household slumped on the settee with blood running from two holes in his neck and soaking into his shirt. More blood ran from a long gash in his arm.

The girls, who appeared to be uninjured, tried to calm their mother while Tony pressed pads on to the lad's neck. I was turning my attention to the mother's arm when we were interrupted by the entrance of her husband.

He was well under the influence of drink and had gone to bed earlier than the rest of the family. So soundly had he been sleeping that he had heard nothing until Satan, confined to the room next to his, had wakened him.

We had enough problems without having to explain what had happened to a man barely able to stand, let alone understand, so I didn't try. Besides I did not know exactly what had happened.

Satan was still snapping and snarling at being confined and one of the girls went to see to him as the ambulance arrived. She had barely opened the door when Satan was through it like a black flash, down the stairs and into the back yard where the ambulance crew had just entered.

He didn't touch them but they looked a little uneasy when they joined us in the living room of the flat. They attended to the injured lad and his mother and we heard the full story.

The son and his mother had been having a disagreement, with the dog looking on. The argument had become quite heated and the mother raised her arm against her son. Satan pounced and seized the mother's arm causing the deep gash I had seen. She screamed and her son tried to beat off the dog.

This further incensed Satan, who released his grip on the mother to snap at the son's arm. He then leapt at the son's face and fastened his jaws around the poor lad's neck.

The concerted efforts of the rest of the family drove off the dog and he was confined to a bedroom.

Next day I went to the shop to see what they intended to do with Satan.

'Had he bitten anyone before last night?'

'Yes, but only members of the family.'

'Why have you kept him if he bites you.'

'He's getting better. When we first had him, about 18 months ago, he was really wild.'

I was glad I had not known Satan when he was 'really wild'.

What would they do with him now?

I pointed out the risks in keeping a large dog that went berserk now and again.

Perhaps the police would like him for training, they suggested. I politely, but firmly, declined.

As far as I know Satan now works for a security firm somewhere in Kent. Kent villains, you have been warned.

John Beaumont *is a PC in Hampshire Constabulary. He is 35, and has three years' service. He is married to Jean, and has a daughter, Andrea, aged nine.*

10 Off the Bus and into the Job

by John Harker

They say the top deck of a bus is the ideal—perhaps the only—way to see London. But I wonder how many people have sat upstairs and decided their destiny. I did.

I had left school in Oxford that lunch-time and was on my way to make final arrangements with the firm I thought was going to be my future employer, a well-known publisher, when the bus stopped outside the county police headquarters.

Before I had time to consider what I was doing, I found myself with cap, scarf and satchel, standing at the inquiry desk saying: 'Please, I want to be a policeman.'

I was ushered into the presence of the recruiting sergeant and, at his invitation, placed my satchel on the floor and myself in a chair and assumed what I imagined to be the look of someone who had decided to dedicate his life to maintaining law and order.

'Well, you had better take the exam,' said the sergeant, thrusting some sheets of foolscap and a question paper towards me.

My first task was to write down, in not fewer than 500 words, what I had done since leaving school. When I pointed out that I had left only half an hour earlier, something between a laugh and a cough came from the direction of a Civil Defence Department constable, sitting in the corner. 'You had better substitute for that why you want to be a policeman, then,' said the sergeant.

How could I stretch to 500 words what had just come to me on a bus 10 minutes earlier? I began to try.

After wading through General Knowledge, bluffing through English and staggering through Maths, I pushed the foolscap sheets back towards the sergeant and gazed out of the window.

'Your Maths are a bit shaky but you've passed.'

'Thank you.'

'Can you come back tomorrow for a medical?'

'Yes,' I replied. 'I'll see you tomorrow then. Goodbye.'

I was outside again in the sunshine ready to resume my journey to the bookshop. I had changed the course of my life before it had even begun. I was 16.

My interview was at the end of July. On August 11, 1958, I was riding my father's pedal cycle to . . . . . . ton Police Station. I was greeted there by the station cleaner, a disappointed-looking, short, round lady with nicotine stains on her moustache. On my entrance she called: 'Vern, someone to see you.'

'Hello. Found your way then?' said Vern.

Rather obvious, I thought.

'Find somewhere to hang your coat.'

I did, and revealed a startling light-blue, double-breasted suit chosen by my mother.

'They haven't given you a uniform yet, then?'

I remember thinking that Vern was going to be quite a conversationalist.

'What do I do?'

'Well,' said Vern. 'Answer the telephone I suppose.'

My mind struggled to grasp the limitless possibilities suggested by this task.

'And put messages in the book.'

Again my brain reeled.

'I'll show you where it is.'

I followed him into the office.

I later discovered Vern wasn't the regular incumbent of the office. He was one of the country policemen holding the fort while Stan, who lived in a War Department bungalow with a pre-war car, took the day off.

About the time that Vern was pointing out to me such necessary pieces of equipment as the telephone switchboard, the coke-boiler (another of my responsibilities) and the telephone book, an ominous figure emerged from a doorway across the yard and stretched and ambled towards me. My sergeant.

He was a tall man with a red face and hair growing on his cheekbones, high up where the razor never reached. He wore no collar and tie and his first action each day was to pick up a brush and begin furiously attacking his trousers, placing one foot at a time on the desk to make it easier to brush their seat.

'Well, John,' he boomed. 'Found your way then?'

Another conversationalist.

'Vern will show you what to do, I'm going to have a shave.' With that he ambled gently back across the yard.

Lil, the cleaner, finished her morning's chores and left. Vern sat at his desk and rustled papers. The sun shone into the yard. The clock ticked. Suddenly the telephone rang . . . 'Police . . . . . . ton,' said Vern. All right, I'll give you the boy.'

He placed the receiver in my trembling hand and said: ' . . . . . . ford with the duties.' I began to take my first steps in learning to be a police cadet. A slow deep voice at the other end began to recite a list of times and places at which various policemen would be available the following day.

'Would you go a little slower please. I'm the new cadet.'

'Oh . . . . . . me!' said the voice, 'all right.'

I proudly replaced the receiver.

'Did you take his name?' asked Vern.

I admitted defeat.

'Well, that was Bill. Always remember to ask their name.'

I mentally grovelled.

The remainder of the day passed uneventfully, apart from tea at 10.30 am and 3 pm (my responsibility again), and lunch—sandwiches on the guardroom table.

I was treated to the awesome sight of George, the CID man, who brought his Yorkshire accent into the station late in the morning, took three enormous drags from a Player's, and ignored me completely.

At 5 pm I was released and rode the 6½ miles home to tea.

'Hello, Mum. I'm back.'

'Found your way then . . . ?'

Life was just beginning.

John Harker *is a Sergeant in Thames Valley Police. He is 40, with 21 years' service and is married with two daughters aged 18 and 16 and one son aged 14.*

11 Freddie Two Sheds

by Bernard Donning

I have never found out how Freddie Two Sheds got his name. Like everything else about Freddie, it was strange.

I met him while working in the plain clothes department. I and another officer, Stevie Corner, had arrested a man and woman on several offences of possessing drugs. After lodging the woman, we took the man, 'Tommy,' back to his flat to search for further drugs. Two other plain clothes officers, Alan Rudd and Trevor Evans, accompanied us.

The flat, in the middle of a low-class council estate, was in poor condition. We had been searching only a few minutes when there was a knock at the front door.

Trevor opened it and there stood Freddie, medium height, thin, dark, curly hair, wide, staring eyes and a large pair of horn-rimmed glasses.

'Come in,' said Trevor. 'Thanks,' said Freddie and walked past him up the hall and into the living room, where the three-piece suite was on its end, the carpet was rolled back, and Stevie was taking pictures off the wall. Tommy sat on a small stool, handcuffed to a radiator. 'All right, Tom?' asked Freddie, as though there was nothing unusual in all this. I don't think it dawned on him what was happening until he was searched.

In his tobacco tin were a small piece of cannabis and an assortment of pills. The only other things he carried were some elastic bands.

Alan and I took Freddie to his flat, on the same estate. I began to search the kitchen, checking the fridge. I turned up four toilet rolls, a loaf, a tin of elastic bands and some blackened vegetable matter. 'What's this?' I asked. 'Magic mushrooms,' said Freddie. 'I dried them under the grill. They keep for ages if you do that.'

I explained the law. 'Oh, well,' he said. 'I'll have to pick some more if you're taking that.' 'What are these doing in the fridge?'—I indicated the elastic bands 'Keeping cool,' he said, looking at me as if I was slightly stupid.

THAT'S STRETCHING IT A BIT FREDDIE.
I'VE

'Why?' I asked. 'It helps the tension.' There was no answer to that. I carried on searching.

Every drawer or cupboard revealed an assortment of pills and lots of elastic bands. I went into the living room and there was Alan, surrounded by more of the same.

'They're all different sizes and give a different tension,' Freddie explained. There were more in the bathroom, the bedroom and the storage cupboard. I was beginning to think he made them.

Boxes full, carrier bags full, there must have been hundreds of thousands. Elastic bands everywhere, plus the usual assortment of pills and a few items of ladies' underwear. (Freddie lived alone. I said he was strange.)

'All right, Freddie.' I said. 'I give up. What are they for?'

'It's private,' he said.

'Have you been pinching them?'

'No.' He looked greatly offended. 'No, I've still got receipts for some of them.'

'All right, but what the hell can you do with thousands of elastic bands?'

'Well, if you really want to know,' said Freddie, 'I wear them. I wear them on my legs, body and arms.' 'Why?' 'You won't believe me.'

'I'm ready to believe almost anything,' I said.

'Well, it's like this,' said Freddie, with an animated expression on his face. 'You put them on various parts of your body and they alter the circulation of your blood. How much depends on the tension you use.'

'And what does that do for you?' 'Helps me to concentrate and get my head together. I used to do it only on my legs, but I'm working my way up.' With that he lifted up his shirt and revealed two large elastic bands digging into his stomach. They looked very painful.

'If you keep working your way up,' I said, 'you'll get your head together with about eight pints of blood in it.'

'I'm very careful,' said Freddie.

Freddie was eventually charged with several offences of possession. He apparently gave a good account of himself at court, telling of his troubles and the depression he suffered. Drugs were his only release.

The magistrates must have been impressed, for he got off with a small fine. Would they have been so lenient if they had seen the bands round Freddie's legs and waist?

Bernard Donning *is a PC in Greater Manchester Police. He is 36, with seven years' service and is married with three children.*

12 Dark Waters

by John Walker

The cinder towpaths were dotted with policemen and civilians, working side by side hauling on the drag-chains. Most of them had gone without sleep and dull eyes seemed to get duller as hope faded with each haul. Winson Green was having a bad day. Three-year-old Sally Greenwood was missing and now, after, two days' searching, we were concentrating on the canal.

I slithered down the steep embankment towards the men below, checking my rate of descent so as not to spill the pot of tea or break any of the cups.

Jim Soaper, the big Lancastrian, dropped his end of the chain and came across to me. His uniform trousers and shirt were filthy, his tie had long been discarded, and his face was streaked with mud and sweat. He managed a tired smile and said, to no one in particular:

'Come on, lads! Tea up.'

I managed to make the tea go round and, as Soapy came for the last cup, I grinned. 'Here y'are mate. Get around that.'

He scratched at his cheek. 'Haven't really got time for this. Still, give it here. Let's get it out of the way.'

Soapy hadn't been home since the morning before, having been first to arrive at the little back house, where Sally had been reported missing. Even then she had been away most of the previous night. Her parents had thought she was with relatives. Since then we had scoured parks, building sites, empty houses and scores of half-demolished buildings. As far as Chief Insp Anson was concerned, time had run out, and reluctantly we had taken out the drag-chains.

Now we were just about finished with the canal, too, having dragged for a good three-quarters of a mile each way from the rear of Sally's house.

Soapy drained the last of his tea and handed me the cup, I threaded it on to the string. 'You ought to jack it in, Soapy,' I said. 'You look done in.'

He wasn't having that. 'Ah'll have me a rest when this little beggar is found and not until.'

I admired his sentiment, but couldn't held feeling that he had things a little twisted. Of course we all wanted to find this little girl, but as it looked now, it wouldn't do her any good. If she was dead now, she would be just as dead when we found her. I hadn't given up hope. There were still a few more houses I could search again. Perhaps my fresh eyes would see something the others had missed.

With the cups jangling on the string, I clambered back up the embankment to the house where I'd been given the tea. There was no one about, so, picking my way across the rubbish-tip of a garden, I left the pot and cups on top of an old mangle and went back to the search.

I was about to go into one of the empty houses, when I noticed the couple from the press. They had been hanging about most of the morning, not exactly getting in the way, but not helping either.

They had walked the banks a score of times, stopping here and there to speak to searchers; choosing the civilians mainly, perhaps feeling they would get more from them. I was thinking they were like a pair of hens scratching about the yard when they headed directly for me. It was my turn, then.

The woman gave me a smile which, in other circumstances, would have seemed engaging, for she really was quite a dish. I soon realised she didn't have the brains to match. Her pencil was hovering over a blank page. 'Any luck yet, officer?' She seemed to be making an effort to sound bright.

I looked at the men toiling below. Feeling that an answer was no more necessary than her question, I shrugged. 'I think we'll find her.'

Her pen got busy and, although I couldn't read shorthand, I could imagine the story in the paper: 'A police spokesman said: "We are *confident*." ' What did it matter? I supposed we would find Sally, eventually.

'What do you think her chances are now?'

I glanced again at the men on the towpath. Another stupid question. 'Well, we are dragging the canal.'

Her companion shifted awkwardly, easing the camera on

his shoulder and the girl flushed slightly. 'Er . . . yes. Well thank you, officer.' This time, she didn't write anything.

Watching them walk away, I sighed again. They had their job to do and I couldn't help feeling a little sorry for them. They had been getting pretty short shrift from the locals and I had the idea that anything the girl wrote would be based more on what she had seen than on what she had heard.

To reach the empty houses, I had to cross a narrow, rubbish-choked feeder canal running along the top of the embankment. Like the main canal, it was heavily silted up and would now contain, at most, three feet of water. The surface was hidden under the thick, green slime on which, as a child, I had thrown pebbles, just to see it break up into tiny islands; islands that slid together again once more, hiding the slick, greasy surface. Even now that slime looked firm enough to walk on.

Of course! To a three-year-old, that's just how that treacherous surface would appear.

Trembling, I walked towards the feeder canal, making for the spot where a worn path met the banks. There had once been a plank across just here, but the makeshift bridge was now in the water, one end beneath the surface, apparently stuck in the silt. On my knees, I leaned across and grabbed the plank and then, using it as a probe, began to feel about beneath the water.

The stink was vile as I disturbed the long-lying mud. Gas bubbling to the surface broke the green film apart and went up my nose. I had covered about 10 yards when I was joined by two local men who, without a word, found themselves a stick each and began to work in the opposite direction.

Almost immediately, one of them stiffened and gasped. 'Oh! No!' Even from where I knelt. I saw the brief flash of red. I could even make out the puckered material, where the elastic ran through the waist of the pantaloons.

I went across and together we lifted the pathetic little bundle on to the bank. We laid her down gently and I felt my eyes begin to prickle. She looked like a little wax doll, slack limbs, sightless eyes gazing upwards.

A small rush of water ran out of her tiny mouth and across the fan of fair hair. I knew I would have to give the pre-arranged signal. But how do you blow a whistle when all you want to do is cry?

John Walker *is a Sergeant in West Midlands Police. He is 44 and has 18 years' service. He is married to Jean, and has two children, Stuart, 12, and Claire, 14.*

13 The Prisoner who came Clean

by John Murgatroyd

Well it finally arrived—the day we had all been dreading. The day Leeds United were to play Glasgow Rangers in an evening 'friendly' match.

Did I say friendly? It turned out to be more like the opening scenario for the Third World War . . .

I was a young patrol sergeant at Millgarth Police Station which covered the central part of the old Leeds City force area.

We had, of course, heard of the extreme patriotism of the Rangers' supporters, and we had been used to large numbers of visitors to the city, for football matches as Leeds were in their prime—so we prepared accordingly.

All police leave was cancelled, extra patrols were organised, men doubled—even trebled in some cases—on the footbeats, all backed up by any form of transport we could lay our hands upon.

Myself and four PCs were detailed to patrol a section of the city centre in a police van. Orders were clear—attend as many incidents as possible and show (if not 'con') the tartan horde that had descended that we were in strength and meant business.

It was a gloriously sunny afternoon and the match wasn't due to start until 7.30 that evening. It seemed that every train, bus and car arrived with an ever increasing number of Scotsmen all wishing to avenge Culloden once and for all.

They filled every pub, cafe, store and other nook or cranny that they could. All were gaily decked out in Rangers' colours or tartan plaid—some even had bagpipes which played at full blast to the terror of the locals.

Calls came thick and fast. 'There's a fight at the Mucky Duck'. 'A couple of Scotsmen have just entered Woolworths—through the display window'. 'A man in a kilt is reported to be doing handstands at the Corn Exchange in front of a bus queue'.

Back and forth went the van. We hardly stopped for breath . . .

"NO LADY, IT'S NOT A SPORRAN"

Then it came. A call which our bemused minds could not register properly. 'Millgarth to patrol in the Boar Lane area—man causing a disturbance at the Griffin Hotel—believed having a bath'. It was the last bit that we could not fully comprehend.

On our arrival at the plush hotel we were greeted by a very distraught assistant manager, splendid in his pinstripe trousers, black jacket, white shirt and tie.

It appeared that one ardent Scottish supporter, who had been celebrating too well in anticipation of his team's victory over the Sassenachs, had paid this salubrious establishment a visit to find some suitable place where he could relieve the pressures of the day's intake.

Finding a toilet on the second floor he had accomplished his mission. There also he had found a nicely fitted bathroom with a large bath which, due to the day's heat and his arm-bending exercises, had proved too attractive to him to ignore. While he was refreshing himself in the warm water the Scot had commenced to render every known song in the football world with a very thick Glaswegian accent.

This naturally had betrayed his presence and brought complaint to the hotel management.

Up the large staircase all five of us went—eager to stop the effrontery to the ears of the guests.

There in the bathroom we were presented by an unforgettable sight—a proud Scot lying in the bath, naked as the day he was born, completely oblivious to the world about him.

No amount of friendly banter brought any recognition of the fact that the law had arrived. Pulling the plug out and allowing the water to drain away did no more than provoke a torrent of unintelligible abuse.

At our request for him to stand up and get dressed, the huge Scot began to take a little notice. With support he stood, slowly and methodically tied his necktie around his neck—but would do nothing else . . .

Thus finding that a diplomatic approach had failed, I decided that we would have to take a more positive action to persuade him to vacate his strategic position.

Grabbing him where we could, we managed to bundle the naked, dripping wet, struggling hunk of Scotch beef out of the bath, on to the second floor landing and past the wide-eyed and astounded female guests who had been attracted by the noise.

We then had to make the perilous journey down the staircase. A pool of water was left at every turn and a cheer was raised by our horizontal load at every step we missed.

Finally, after what seemed an hour, we managed to load the struggling tie-bedecked mass into the police van, shut the doors to the gaze of the world, and head for the Bridewell leaving our embarrassment behind.

Needless to say there was one Scotsman less at the match that night but this was compensated when we allowed him to return to his green hills of home much cleaner than when he came.

John Murgatroyd *is a Sergeant in West Yorkshire Metropolitan Police. He is 47, has 27 years' service and is married with two sons aged 24 and 22. His eldest son is also a police officer in West Yorkshire.*

14 The Reluctant Prisoner

by Colin Macdonald

I knew as soon as she walked into the police station that this was going to be a 'red-inker', and that I would be handpicked from a short list of one to deal with it.

The lady in question was one who, with her common-law husband, had achieved some small notoriety for the volume and frequency of their domestic disputes (the area was one where these things were appreciated).

No 'advice given' job this; she had a real beauty of a black eye, the sort that could not be ignored, even by those with the most selective eye-sight.

As I had thought, I got to deal with it. Despite being the smallest officer, and at that time the most junior, I somehow managed to get to the front of the queue of those eagerly waiting to take the matter on.

And so a statement of complaint was taken by me from the lady whose injury was duly photographed and a posse comprising a sergeant, a policewoman and myself travelled to the matrimonial abode to have words with the common-law husband.

Now both he and the aggrieved were partial to the old jungle juice and, as luck would have it, the accused was in bed sleeping it off after a session. We were let into the house by the youngest child and taken to his recumbent parent.

Our quarry was in bed wearing a tee-shirt, underpants and nothing else and soon made it clear that he had no intention of coming with us to the police station.

He indicated this by his adamant refusal to put on his trousers and his gentle suggestion to Sandy, the policewoman, that she should 'get back to the sink and wash your pots, woman'.

Sandy then left the room while the sergeant and I remained to persuade the prisoner to 'be a good chappie and please put his flipping trousers on if it wasn't too much trouble'. He wouldn't and, although we did try, we couldn't.

Nor would he walk downstairs with us. Given the choice of

"HIS FEET HAVE ATE HIS ODOUR EATERS"

that or being manhandled out he chose the latter. And so we carried him, face up and horizontal, semi-nude and paralytic, bump, bump, bump down the stairs.

This man was no lightweight and, after leaving via the front door, we suggested that he might like to walk to the nearby panda car; but no, he gave us advice on sex and travel, indicating that he preferred to be carried.

This was 'not on'. I was only slightly built, Sandy had suffered enough from the close proximity of the prisoners's smelly feet and Vick, the sergeant, clearly had no intention of going on a medical so close to retirement.

We elected to drag him. As luck would have it the children did not make much use of the garden gate, preferring entry to the family estate via the more convenient hole in the front hedge. We chose this route also as the shortest between the house door and the police vehicle.

An audience of neighbours looked on as we dragged the prisoner by his smelly feet over the 'lawn' and through the gap in the hedge. He was still dressed only in his tee-shirt and y-fronts and was telling us in his quaint Anglo-Saxon vocabulary what fond memories he would always have of the Nottinghamshire Constabulary, and what jolly nice people we all were.

We eventually managed to pull the prisoner through the front hedge and, after a 10 yard scrape along the pavement on his bare back, he finally indicated that perhaps he would favour travelling in the vertical position after all.

Our kindly natures, and the obvious fact this man did not make frequent use of foot deodorant, allowed him this privilege and we duly arrived without further incident at the police station.

The prisoner was shown the 'guest accommodation' and the inspector was informed of his arrival.

The inspector joined us and was told that the prisoner was not amenable to interview. Undeterred, and claiming to be on good terms with the offender, whom he had met previously, the inspector decided to speak to the man himself.

He emerged some five minutes later, looking less than successful, and embarked on a conversation with Sandy and myself which soon came round to the prisoner's dishevelled physical appearance.

I glanced at Sandy and—no I couldn't resist it—'Looks like he's been dragged through a hedge backwards, doesn't he, Sir?'

Colin Macdonald *is a PC in Nottinghamshire Police. He is 30, and has eight years' service. He is married to Paula, and has a daughter, Claire, aged four.*

15 An Angel's Promise

by John Chapman

He was known as 'Angel Face', and that was the only part of him that was angelic. He had shot his way out of hold-ups that went wrong, escaped from every form of detention, from police cell to high-risk security prisons, and he was on the run again. It was known that he kept a loaded .38 revolver in the dash of the car and an axe with a three-feet handle in the boot. He had vowed he would not be taken again.

His wife and kids had been rehoused from 'The Smoke' to Basildon new town. The Divisional Detective Inspector 'Trunkie' (so-called because he had the proboscis that went with the ability to smell out bandits) reckoned Angel Face would take his chances and visit his family over the forthcoming Christmas holiday. We'd have twenty-four hour surveillance on the property Christmas Day and Boxing Day. After that, 'we'll see'.

All the detectives in the division were called in for the operation. Those stationed outside Basildon Town would take the day observations, and the Basildon officers the nights, so they could be with their families during the day. Well, charity always starts at home.

At the time I was a DC stationed at a section, Wickford, on the outskirts of Basildon, so Christmas Day and Boxing Day were going to be full of fun for me. The wife wasn't very pleased either. 'That's right, put the job before your family. Out drinking with your pals. It doesn't matter about me and the kids.' If I had told her the truth, that there was a good chance she would be drawing a police widow's pension in the New Year, she wouldn't have believed me.

The suspect house was one of a terrace in a square, with a large green between it and the road. What a way to spend Christmas Day! Still, with a bit of luck he wouldn't come. Some clever sod checked out all the cars around the square. One, a large Ford Zodiac, had been stolen from the Met. He was here, all right.

If we made a frontal attack, with a woman and young

ER...ER...EARLY MORNING CALL ...ER... SIR.

children in the house and anything happened to them, we would be held responsible.

By the way, did I mention that this was a time when the only firearms the police had were kept in the museum at Headquarters, and had been used by some guy called Brown or Kennedy back in the Twenties? All we had was a truncheon and a smooth line in patter. Angel Face was unlikely to be impressed.

Another clever Dick—why didn't I think like them?—worked out that if, under cover of darkness, the air was let out of the rear offside tyre of the Ford, matey would be forced to change the wheel when he came out. While he remained poised between dashboard and boot we would rush him, and at least have some chance of remaining alive. Brilliant; but the bloke who thought of the idea didn't have to let the tyre down. Delegation, the key to success.

Boxing Day passed. Nothing. He had to come out sometime, so carry on the observation.

About 7am the following day a figure came across the green like a bat out of Hell, into the Ford, started first time, and away. Who didn't let enough air out of the tyre? He was going like the hammers. The little CID car with three inside had little chance of catching him. He was getting further away every minute. He reached the A127 Southend—London arterial road, making for London, and our chances of catching him looked even slimmer.

But don't give me a clever man, give me a lucky one. At the first petrol station just past the Fortune of War public house he pulled in. As he stood at the pump the CID car puffed in to the forecourt. Fall out the guard. I won't say it was easy, but he was nicked. He didn't like it one little bit.

When Trunkie went over to visit him in the cell Angel Face went berserk, foaming at the mouth, and between obscenities making the point that to take a man when he was visiting his wife and family at Christmas was unwelcome, unprincipled and ought to be unlawful. It was neither the time nor the place to mention the slight inconvenience he had caused us.

His last words to Trunkie before leaving Basildon were to the effect that he would not forget the matter, and when he got out he would remove Trunkie from the land of the living.

About three years later I was stationed at Pitsea, still in the Basildon division, to which I had been promoted as uniform sergeant. The station adjoined a row of county-owned police houses, the end one of which was occupied by Trunkie and his wife. As befitted a man of officer rank, he had an extension from his house to the switchboard at Pitsea nick, so that he could call and be called at all hours of the day and night.

By this time firearms were beginning to be held at divisional stations, and had to be signed for after obtaining authority from Headquarters. They were kept in the Divisional Chief Superintendent's office under lock and key. That is, his key, so it was hard luck if he didn't happen to be about when you needed one, even if you did have the authorisation.

It was also at this time that Angel Face made his umpteenth escape. The powers-that-be had been so impressed with his assurance that he would get Trunkie that they allowed Trunkie to carry a loaded .38 revolver on duty at all times. It was also arranged that if the flap on the Pitsea switchboard from his extension at home was flickered it meant that trouble had arrived and we should take what action was required—whatever that meant. At least Angel Face's promise was not being taken lightly.

On this particular day I was the early-turn skipper, on at 6am. I had done the important jobs—had a mug of tea, sorted out as much paperwork as I could pass over to the late-turn sergeant—and was out in the station yard putting some pumped air into the county bike before setting off to make a few points with the patrol lads. The office man came out in a rush, white-faced. 'Trunkie's flap's just gone up and down,' he blurted out.

My mind immediately went back to that Christmas. Inform Division and then do something. But what?

Young Collyer had his own .410 shotgun in the boot of his car, so I told him to cover Trunkie's back door with it while I went and knocked on the front one. There wasn't much else I could do; he was the only man I had available at the time.

I wished that I carried my truncheon on early turn, but it did drag the side of your trousers down when cycling to make the points, so it was safe at home in the kid's playpen. I wished I was with it as I knocked on the door. No reply. It's true a coward dies a hundred deaths; I can speak from experience.

I banged again. A long pause, then the door was opened a few inches by Mrs Trunkie in her night clothes and dressing gown. She looked a bit startled. Was Angel Face standing behind the door waiting to blast me to Kingdom Come, or perhaps the other place?

'Can I see the DI?' I asked. 'Well, it's not convenient at the moment. Can't it wait?' she said.

Blimey, he's holding them hostage, I thought.

'I'm afraid it can't', I told her (I'm afraid was right, anyway.)

'Oh well,' she said, and disappeared, leaving the door ajar. I pushed it open and ran into the passageway, just in time to see the DI, silver hair all over the place, no teeth, shaving soap all over his chin, coming down the stairs in vest and trousers.

'You all right, Guv? Your flap just went on the switchboard.'

He nodded in the direction of his wife: 'That silly cat knocked the receiver off walking past it.'

'I put it back straight away,' she said.

'I know you did,' I agreed. Trunkie knew without my saying anything.

'Thanks, John,' he said, and that to me was worth more than any chief constable's commendation. 'And thank whoever was on the switchboard,' he added.

By the time I returned to the station there were area cars, traffic cars, men on motor-cycles and men on push bikes all milling about in the station yard.

'False alarm,' I said, all cocky, like. 'Back to work, lads.' Then I went in the station and made the tea.

Angel Face? I see him now and then on television, an authority imparting his wisdom through the media whenever there has been a particularly nasty shoot-out or prison break. He speaks now like a latter-day saint, or even Brian Clough.

I bet he doesn't remember the time he fouled up my Christmas.

16 The story of Ada

by Anne Williams

As far as I know she is still alive so I will call her Ada Tuffy. Ada was an elderly, alcoholic midget.

The only herald of her arrival at the front desk in Maidstone Police Station was a cruising navy blue hat, made of straw and bedecked with artificial fruit, just above the counter.

Her face was cratered with age and her mouth was toothless; she wore a coat that had once been cream coloured which almost met her wrinkled stockings at the ankles, and scuffed, toe-less shoes; she shuffled rather than walked and had amazing balance—the angles to the ground she could achieve and still manage to regain the vertical were incredible.

Her constant companions were an extremely battered shopping bag, a bottle of anything alcoholic but usually sherry, and her glass eye.

No particular reason ever prompted Ada's visit to the station but she would attempt to tell anyone who would listen that youths were calling her names or that she had no money to get home.

Even her arrival to consult the police was somewhat miraculous as the route was mined with such things as Pelican crossings, kerbs and supermarket trolleys, all of which took some negotiating through an alcoholic haze.

In the past I had often recovered Ada from the middle of a busy pavement or the edge of the road where she had gently lain down to sleep off the effects of a day's liquid intake.

She did not ask much and would angrily wave away the attentions of passers-by who were, understandably, concerned for the small, fairly evil-smelling human snoozing peacefully in the middle of the precinct.

Ada was, like so many of her kind, apparently friendless and without family. She would drift into our town from the countryside every so often and then we would not see her for

HIC... AND I'VE GOT TURNUPS IN MY KNICKERS.. HIC

months. I believe she lived at a homeless persons' hostel but I never managed what you would class as conversation with her to find out—even her sober state was a trifle jumbled.

On this particular occasion Ada's speech was sufficiently incoherent for me to abandon leaning suspended over the counter in order to hear her and go to the door for a closer confrontation.

I opened the door just in time to watch her self-righting mechanism fail and she went, in slow motion and absolutely straight, crashing backwards on to the stone floor, followed in a split second by the explosion of her full bottle and a slick of sticky brown sherry gradually surrounded her inert form. Ada was paralytic, out for the count.

With the aid of a colleague I carried Ada, complete with hat and bag, to the cells. A preliminary examination found no obvious damage to her person; her totally relaxed, alcohol-induced state had saved her from serious injury. She lay snoring loudly, a beatific smile on her face.

Deciding that nothing but time could render her as near normal as possible, I made her reasonably comfortable, adjusted her on to her side and then, reluctantly, began to list the contents in the dubious interior of the shopping bag.

After putting on a pair of transparent gloves I delved into the sticky depths, withdrew a few coins, a mountain of used and unused tissues and the bottom of the sherry bottle. My hand then gently closed on a soft, oval object, roughly the size of a hen's egg.

At this stage it must be said that I had not actually looked Ada straight in the face that day. My chat with her over the counter had been rather conspiratorial, she whispering in my ear and me making what I hoped were the appropriate noises.

On opening the door she had keeled over so, problem: did she or did she not have her glass eye in? I looked over to her sleeping form and, frankly, could not bring myself to prise open the lids of her wrinkled old eyes.

I knew from experience that if I asked for help I would never live it down. Thinking brave thoughts I withdrew my hand from the bag, clutching the oval object. By now I was utterly convinced that I was holding Ada's glass orbit and wondered, vaguely, whether it would wink at me.

Gingerly, I unravelled the tissue surrounding it and gazed down on a perfectly peeled hard-boiled egg, the uneaten remnant of her picnic lunch.

Anne Williams *retired from Kent County Constabulary as a WPC after 10 years' service. She is 30, and married with a baby daughter.*

17 Silent O'Toole and Supermouth

by Keith Clegg

O'Toole had all the grace and charm, not to mention the height, of a grizzly bear. He had been employed on various building sites in the area as a hod-carrier's mate, but he was not matey by nature. Indeed few people had heard him say a word. He was a loner, mysterious.

By all accounts, O'Toole was a conscientious worker. At the end of a hard day, he would return to his one-roomed flat, wash and shave, put on his best cap, coat and boots, and then go out on the town.

He would walk into the first pub that took his fancy, commandeer a space at the bar, consume pints until he was as drunk as Father Murphy's pig, and then toddle off home.

He kept himself to himself, picked on no one and no one picked on him. The nearest O'Toole came to trouble was when, one night in one of his regular haunts, he was making his way somewhat unsteadily towards the gents. He fell over the landlord's dog just in front of the door. O'Toole gave it such a stare that it scampered off, whimpering and trembling, for the shelter of the nearest table, from under which it refused to move for the following three-and-a-half hours.

Round about this time, there was, in our division, a young copper who had just enough service in to get his chin-strap wet, but still knew everything and had done everything. 'Supermouth' had completed his probation and had attended classes and courses until he had mnemonics, wall charts and definitions running out of his ears. He was supremely confident of passing his sergeant's exams that year (again), and had even bought a Road Atlas of Great Britain so he could plot the quickest overland route to Bramshill.

Supermouth was a very good theorist, but when it came down to practical policing, he tended to over-react or grasp the wrong end of the stick, and sometimes, to put it diplomatically, he made a complete cock-up. He hadn't a clue, he lacked judgement, and nobody liked him. Indeed, we all had to admit, he was excellent officer material.

On the debit side, he was a clown. He played the most

idiotic pranks on people, especially on nights. We tried to warn him, but he just would not listen. He was far too smart to be caught out by anybody, or so he thought.

He used to waylay unsuspecting drunks and harangue them with shouts of, 'Vott are you doink on zer streets? Are you not avare off ze curfew? Vott iz your name, vank and number, you British schvine?'

Another of his tricks was to rush up to the first solitary inebriate he could find, and ask, in a breathless stammer:

'Excuse me, sir. Have you seen a ca, ca, ca, car? It's a Fo, Fo, Fo, For, For, For . . . '

'Ford?' the drunk would venture.

'No. A Vauxhall,' he would snap back, and then continue:

'It's colour is gra, gra, gree, gree . . . '

'Green?' the drunk would ask.

'No. It's red,' he would reply. And so on and so on.

Eventually he would conclude the conversation: 'Thank you very much, Sir. You've been most helpful.' Then he would jump back into his car, and drive off, leaving his victim foaming at the mouth.

It became Supermouth's dearest wish to waylay O'Toole with one of his jolly japes, but he always missed him, or was sent on a job, just when he had the fellow in his sights. But he needn't have worried, destiny was bound to throw them together. As John Wayne would have said, 'This town ain't big enough for the both of us'.

It's doubtful whether their meeting, when it came, did anything for O'Toole, but it certainly made a changed man out of Supermouth.

He had parked one night, to make some notes in his duty diary, when a noise made him look up. There was O'Toole, staggering up the street towards the police car. Even when he had a drunken smile on his lips, O'Toole had a face full of menace.

Supermouth got out and stood a few feet in front of his prey. Then he began his routine.

'Excuse me, Sir,' he began . . .

'I'm looking for a car. It's a Fo, Fo, Fo, Fo, . . . Ford.'

He stopped short. O'Toole was staring at him, expressionless.

Supermouth tried again. 'It's colour is wy, wy, wu, wu, white'.

O'Toole shambled forwards and, reaching out with fingers like a bunch of hairy bananas, clamped them tightly around Supermouth's throat. The tips of their noses came within half an inch of each other.

Then, as O'Toole began to shake hands with Supermouth's windpipe, he spoke those unforgettable words: 'Are you troying' ter be fa, fa, fa, fa, fa, fa, funny?'

Keith Clegg *is a PC in Lancashire Constabulary. He is 43 and has 15 years' service. He is married with a son of 13 and a daughter of 11.*

18 Where's the Fire?

by Ian Smith

It was 1.45 am. I stretched my arms and legs in an effort to stir up enough energy to leave the canteen and get back on duty. That cake was a bit on the dry side. Perhaps next Christmas my wife could make one that would not last through the year.

I stood up, buttoned my tunic and packed my paperback on divining into my grub bag. The others began to arrive, armed with cards and crib boards. I left and went downstairs into the communications room.

'You just going out?' asked the Sergeant.

'Good. Just had a call from the fire brigade. They're going to a cooker fire at No. 13 Marine Parade.'

'At this time of the morning?'

'Seems so,' he said, as I left to find the panda.

I got to Marine Parade as fast as my 1.1 Escort would allow and found that the brigade had beaten me. (I am sure they wait till they've got a good start before telling us.) Marine Parade was a terrace of old properties of at least four storeys. The front doors opened out into one of the main routes into town and the road at this point was part of a one-way system.

I parked and walked towards No. 13. As I reached the door three firemen came out and told me that it was a malicious call. In the absence of any fire, their enthusiasm was quickly extinguished and in next to no time they had packed up and left for their still warm bunks—leaving a puzzled policeman on the doorstep.

Then the owner of the property appeared. He saw me and immediately beckoned with both arms. 'Come in, come in. There is something I must tell you.'

I detected an accent and sure enough the gentleman turned out to be of Polish origin, having settled in this country after the war. His name was Mr Stepowski. I followed him into his house. Up and up we went, to the top floor. He led me to a bedroom, pointed to the ceiling, and said: 'Look. Look at that.' I looked. There was a large dirty patch in what was otherwise a white ceiling. 'What happened?' I asked.

'I want to 'ave this 'ole mended, so I gets this builder along to fix it. He tells me it costs £50 to do and that 'e needs £25 now for raw materials. I gave 'im the money but 'e did not come. After a long time, 'e comes for two hours and does this. It's terrible!' He pointed to the ceiling again in utter despair.

'Did you pay him the rest of the money?'

'No. I told 'im that it was so terrible and in the end 'e agreed not to charge me the other £25.'

I couldn't blame him.

'But, now I have started to get these phone calls. The builder says 'e wants the rest of the money.'

I asked him for the builder's name but before he could answer, the telephone rang downstairs. This was too much for the poor man. He threw his arms in the air and started shouting: 'It's 'im, it's 'im.'

We ran downstairs and into the living room. 'You answer it,' he said.

What did he expect me to say? 'This is a policeman. If that is the builder, I think your work on Mr Stepowski's ceiling should be designated a disaster area'?

But I picked up the receiver and sheepishly said hello. A voice asked: 'Mr Stepowski?' 'Yes,' I said. The caller hung up.

Before I had time to replace the receiver Mr Stepowski said: 'You see. It's 'im, the builder. Oh! What can I do?' I had to agree he had a problem.

'Do you know who this builder is?'

'Well, I don't know 'is name but I 'ave . . . ' He broke off as the phone rang again. 'You answer it! Oh! what shall I do?'

I picked up the receiver. As soon as I said hello the phone went dead.

Mr Stepowski was becoming visibly weak at the knees. 'You go and make a cup of tea,' I told him. I had a feeling this so-called 'cooker fire' was becoming a trifle involved. I tried desperately to recall a suitable paragraph from the 19th edition of *Moriaty*. Should I perhaps send Mr Stepowski to see his friendly solicitor? Who was this mysterious builder, anyway?

The phone interrupted by thoughts and Mr Stepowski came

running back in with a teapot. Without waiting for his invitation, I picked up the receiver and said, in my finest Polish, ''Ello. Who ees dat?'

'It's the builder. Who's speaking?'

'This is Mr Stepowski speaking,' I said.

'Now listen,' he answered. 'You had better give me the 25 quid you owe me. I've been watching you and I know which way you go to work and come home. Give me the money or else.'

Bells started ringing in my brain. *Moriarty* was telling me the builder was making an unwarranted demand with menaces. With added confidence, I said, 'All right, I'll give you the money. What do you wish me to do?'

The voice said: 'Put it in an envelope and leave it in a milk bottle in the crate on next door's doorstep. Do you understand?'

I said I did.

The voice continued: 'We will be along in 15 minutes to collect the money.'

I replaced the receiver and paused to gather my thoughts. Mr Stepowski was quiet and staring at me. I reached for my PR and called the station. 'Panda 6 to Echo'.

'Go ahead', came the merry reply.

'This should get them going,' I thought. 'I have a slight problem concerning the fire call you sent me to at No. 13 Marine Parade.' I explained the events of the last 30 minutes. After I had finished, there was an awkward pause.

'Call you back Panda 6', came their reply. Time was pressing and I told Mr Stepopwski to place some strips of newspaper in an envelope. I then watched him go outside into Marine Parade and deposit the envelope in the milk crate next door.

Comms room called me back. The inspector and sergeant, they said, were concealing themselves in some bushes opposite Mr Stepowski's house. Feeling slightly relieved that they had, so far, taken me seriously, I decided to leave.

My panda was still parked outside. If the builder was already nearby and watching the premises it might scare him off.

Not wishing to take any chances, I explained the danger to

Mr Stepowski and he came out into Marine Parade with me. We shook hands, waved, shouted pleasant farewells and I drove away, trying to remain cool, calm and collected, just as they tell us at training school.

I concealed the car at a discreet distance from Marine Parade, switched off the engine, and enjoyed the peace and quiet. I thought of the inspector and sergeant in the bushes. If our builder didn't turn up I wouldn't be very popular. The radio crackled. 'Echo to Panda 6. Go back to Marine Parade.'

I raced back to find the inspector and sergeant with not one, but three prisoners, plus a local taxi driver. The inspector told me to take a statement from Mr Stepowski and directed the taxi driver to take prisoners and escorts back to the station.

I spent the next hour or more taking the statement. It was only when I returned to the station that I found out the other side of the story. It transpired that the builder and his wife had been at a party. The builder decided the time had come to collect the remaining cash from the unfortunate Mr Stepowski. He had made the fire call and the other three. After the third call, he had hired a taxi and left the party for Marine Parade with his wife and a friend who just came along for the ride.

As I had feared, on arriving at Mr Stepowski's, they saw my panda. Undaunted, they told the taxi driver to go round the block until I had left. After my departure they had stopped the taxi and collected the envelope, only to be instantly arrested.

This 'farce', as our legal branch later referred to it, resulted in the builder's appearance (and conviction) at Crown court on a charge (Hurrah for *Moriarty's* 19th Edition) of blackmail.

Ian Smith *is a PC in Sussex Police. He is 30 and has had 11 years' service. He is married with two children, Ben aged 10 and Claire aged seven.*

19 He Who Laughs Last

by Michael Hirst

I was a sergeant in the traffic department at the time, in those halcyon days when enforcement was the sole policing objective and transgressors were regarded as anti-social and left in no doubt about it.

I was driving home from early turn, having just finished my third quick change on the rota before the weekend off. Nothing had a more destructive effect on my constitution than the 10 pm finish followed by a 6 am start. And the one week each month when the rota necessitated three of those shifts left me a shadow of my professional self and positively evil with it.

The road home was a main arterial route out of Leeds. I was approaching the brow of a fairly steep hill in my aging Rover 90 saloon, directly behind a shiny, new 3.8 Jaguar saloon. Half-way up the hill the Jag slowed down so that the driver could exercise his curiosity on the burnt-out shell of a lorry in a nearby field, which had been a victim of the treacherous hill a few days earlier.

Now, whether it was the spate of late/early shifts, or that his Jag was shinier than my Rover, or that, by slowing down, my old car would require first gear to get to the top of the hill, I shall never know. But I decided that the driver was not exercising due care and attention and would have to be told. A verbal warning should suffice.

He was almost stationary, but it was with considerable difficulty and clouds of blue smoke that I managed to overtake him. I stopped on the brow of the hill, grabbed my cap, jumped out and, resplendent in full uniform, froze the Jag with a number one signal that would have stopped Hannibal.

I went over to him and started a fairly moderate routine roasting, referring to his slowing down without signals, obstructing other traffic and not giving proper consideration to other road users.

To my surprise he tried to interrupt me before I had even finished Act I, Scene One. I told him to shut up and listen. I continued to point out to him his social responsibility as a driver and how a little forethought could prevent accidents and save lives.

To my astonishment he again tried to interrupt, this time gesticulating wildly up the road. I was hardened to this type of distraction. I had done two years as a military policeman, six as a City policeman and three late/early shifts. He stood no chance. I gave him both barrels. I was even subconsciously considering my powers of arrest when I sensed victory. He settled in his seat, smiled sardonically and was obviously prepared to wait until I had finished, which I just about had.

He then thanked me for my advice and, as I stood up, still fixing him with a stare and notching another mental triumph, he played his trump: 'I was only trying to tell you, sergeant, that your car is running away.'

Even before I turned round, I knew that, in my haste, I had omitted to set the handbrake. As I looked to where the Rover had been, I could just see the top of its grey roof disappearing down the other side of the hill.

In the 40 yards it took me to catch the car, open the door, and ignominously clamber inside, my imagination ran riot. I could visualise the 30 cwt motor running amok and crashing through houses, shops and factories all at the expense of my no-claims bonus. Fortunately, binding brakes, a lack of servicing in general and an absence of grease in particular prevented rapid acceleration.

As I brought the car under control, the Jag passed me. To say that the driver was in hysterics would be an understatement. I realised why when I went to collect my cap, which I had lost in the chase. He had run over it. I think the 18 shillings I had to pay for a new one hurt me most.

20 Search me Guv

by Alan Wheeler

Our sectional station on the outer fringes of the Met was a happy little nick. The station garden was a delight and we usually won the annual competition. We policed a working-class neighbourhood with the usual cross-section of honest artisans and sundry willains.

Uniform and CID worked as a team and so long as the arrests came in the station sergeant (we didn't rate an inspector) didn't worry too much if we spent an extra 10 minutes or so on our refreshments and a game of solo.

One morning I had a telephone call from an informant (come to think of it, he was probably my only informant in those days). 'Can you get a warrant for 29 Drake Road?' he asked.

'Sure—what's in there?'

'Nothing at the moment—just get a warrant.'

Now, in those days you didn't have to specify what you were looking for, so I toddled off to our local court and laid on information for 'stolen property'.

A few days went by and I still had the warrant in my pocket. I daren't put it in the warrant register, for when our somewhat irascible detective superintendent next visited he would have wanted to know why it hadn't been executed.

Weeks went by and I had almost forgotten it. Then one morning the local tallyman found his shop had been completely cleaned out—which didn't please him as he had only just had his winter stock delivered *and* he wasn't insured. The other DC and I went round and did the necessary but it was a glove job and no one had heard or seen a thing.

No sooner had we got back to the nick when the phone rang.

'Have you still got the "W" for Drake Road?'

'Yes. Why?'

'I should get round there pretty quick.'

Putting two and two together, I grabbed a few of the lads from the canteen and when we got there I sent three of them round the back while my mate and I knocked on the front door. After too long a time dear old Mum answered and we were met with the usual torrent of abuse (the family was not exactly unknown to us).

The first thing we saw was that the front room had some additional furniture, in the shape of two camp beds, and the sheets were still warm. When we went upstairs we saw the reason: two of the bedrooms were full (and I mean full, floor to ceiling) with the proceeds of the tallyman's shop.

Proceedings were interrupted by three helmetless constables with an armlock on one of the sons of the house, who was limping slightly. Both the boys had done a bunk through a back window. One had got away.

Mum by this time was putting on the usual song and dance routine, now aided and abetted by various neighbours who had come to join in the fun.

I told the arresting officers to take son and heir back to the station, search him, and put him in the detention room while we sat on the property. This was duly done and his property (the usual five Woodbines, one box of matches and a few coppers) was listed in the back of the charge book.

Eventually the van appeared and we loaded the property—everything from napkins to nappies, raincoats to rompers. It took three van loads before all was safely gathered in.

A few hours later it was time to question our friend occupying the guest room. He couldn't wriggle out of this one and anyway he was fond of his Mum and wouldn't like her charged with receiving.

I unlocked the detention room door. The prisoner was sitting on the chair with both elbows on the table, on which was a spanking new 4ft jemmy.

'What the hell is that doing there?'

'Don't know, Guv. It must belong to the station cleaner.'

Then I remembered his limp. He must have stuck it down his trouser leg before beating his hasty retreat.

'You realise you'll be stuck on for another charge of possessing HBI by day?'

'That's up to you. But your boys searched me and they wrote it all down in the book, *and* I signed my name that the property was correct. So did the officer.'

The arresting officer was a nice young lad and it was his first arrest for a crime. At the very least he was due for a rocket for not properly searching the prisoner.

So if anyone wants a 4ft jemmy, only one owner, hardly used and free of charge, I can show them exactly where it is. The village duckpond is still there.

Alan Wheeler *retired from the Metropolitan Police as a Detective Chief Inspector after 25 years' service. He is 55 and married.*

21 Two's a Crowd

by Tony Boyes

We have area constables these days and community policemen. Well, in the County force I joined . . .ty years ago, we had village policemen. These people knew everyone and everything that happened on their patch.

I was in my early twenties, with a younger wife, and a baby a few weeks old, when I became a village policeman. At least I thought I did. I realise now that I never really made it . . . because of Fred.

Fred was the epitome of the comic village bobby: 6ft tall, red, round face, round stomach, small amount of grey hair, moustache. He wore cycle clips—all the time. He was never out of uniform. Even on his day off he wore police trousers . . .

He was the policeman in the next village and before I had arrived had covered my beat for years. He knew as much about my couple of villages and hamlets as he did about his own kingdom. The result was that my villagers told me nothing. They barely acknowledged my existence.

Fred would call at my station on his way to 'supervise' my village. The conversation would go something like this:

Fred: 'How's it going on then?'

Me: 'Oh, mustn't grumble . . . '

Very little happened there, apart from road accidents. Fred wasn't always about at the time so they fell to me to deal with. And there was the occasional sudden death.

I would have the odd crime to investigate. Once there was a burglary. Some money had been stolen. I made inquiries. The locals told me nothing. Fred came along, they answered his questions, but the crime went undetected.

I have one admission to make. On rare days off the only way to escape from the job was to disappear for the day. I was returning to my village after one of these breaks when I saw the remains of a road accident. I accelerated, driving straight past as though I didn't belong there. I admit now a feeling of guilt. On my return to the village about half an hour later, I did see Fred, notebook in hand, helmet on the back of his head, taking details in his pocket-book.

Of course when Fred was on his day off, I would cover his village, or pretend to.

About 3 am one spring morning I was awakened by the telephone alongside my bed.

'County Police . . . ' I answered.

'Divisional Office 'ere. There's a barn on fire up at —ton. Fred's on day off. Will you turn out?'

He meant 'You will', and so I did.

Right, I thought. I've got you, Fred. This time I'll deal with something you'll know nothing about.

So, contrary to force orders, I got out my car, a Ford Popular, three-geared model, 1172 cc with strange suspension. I dashed off at full speed 48 mph, up the main road. I could see the flames in the distance. Glory was mine.

I arrived within a few hundred yards to be waved down by someone with a torch. A mystic figure in black, cape and helmet.

I pulled to a stop. 'Ullo. What you doin' 'ere?' asked Fred.

'I've been called by —bury,' I told him. 'They told me you were on day off.'

'Ah, so I might be, but one of my locals called me.'

I appreciated his help. It was a losing battle. Maybe I was a bit young for this village bobby lark . . . I gave up after that.

Tony Boyes *is a Sergeant in Thames Valley Police, working in the Press Office. He is 48 and has had 28 years' service. He is married to Sylvia, has a married daughter, Susan, and two sons, Stuart, 21, and Alexander, 11.*

22 A Slow Streak

by David Williams

I didn't take any notes at the time. I had no notebook. I was half way through a three-year law course at Liverpool University. Studying the judgments of Lord Denning. And others. No involvement with police work for 18 months.

I had left the Faculty at about four that afternoon and was driving home along Renshaw Street. A busy city centre road. Full of traffic and people. On glancing to my right I thought I saw a coloured man climbing out of his trousers on the pavement on the other side of the road.

I rubbed my eyes, and looked again. I did see a coloured man climbing out of his trousers on the pavement on the side of the road.

He then started walking along the pavement in the opposite direction to me. Just walking at a normal pace, naked as the day he was born, as though it were the most natural thing to do in a busy city street in the middle of the afternoon.

The varied reactions of passers-by were an education. Many—no doubt having been brought up in the British tradition of it being rude to stare—were pointedly looking everywhere except at him. Others were looking right through him as though they hadn't even noticed that he was there.

Young girls standing in bus queues giggled as he passed. A fair number of people looked annoyed and angry. But nobody made any protest or did anything to stop him.

'You're a policeman,' I said to myself, 'it's up to you.' But I was a student as well, and didn't want to get involved with police work if it could be avoided. Future court cases could clash with important lectures.

I know, I'll drive round the block and find a policeman. With a bit of luck it might be a policewoman. I'd like to see her reaction when I asked her to get in my car to chase a naked man.

But it's true what they say. You can never find one when you want one. So it was still down to me.

I drove around the block until I was following him up

"COR BLIMEY! IT'S TRUE"
LFC
ETTE
LIVERPOOL

Renshaw Street. I pulled up in front of him, got out of the car and walked back towards him. He was still walking at a normal pace. No attempt to run.

I flashed my warrant card. 'What are you doing?' I inquired.

'I'm streaking,' he confided in an everyday conversational tone, as though this was a normal pastime. (And I had always thought that speed was inherent to the concept of streaking. You live and learn.)

I explained the error of his ways, and told him that he was under arrest for insulting behaviour.

'This is it,' I thought. 'This is where he gets violent and I end up rolling around in the middle of the roadway, wrestling with a naked man.'

But, no. He acquiesced with a quiet 'OK'. This is obviously what he had wanted in the first place.

Now what to do with him? No way was I going to walk him through the streets. I led him to my Austin Maxi and put him in the back seat, with the child safety lock on for security.

I took him to the nearest police station, which happened to be Force HQ. They have no facilities for prisoners there, but the quicker I got him out of the car the better in case he had a go at me while I was driving.

I pulled outside the main entrance in Hope Street. I thought that for modesty's sake I better get him some covering before I took him in. There were women about who might have had delicate feelings about being confronted with a naked man.

I waved through the glass doors to the duty constable behind the public inquiry desk. He waved back and carried on writing. I gesticulated wildly towards the back of the car and finally got his attention again.

He came from behind the desk and opened the entrance door. Had he a uniform mac, I asked. Ah! a look of understanding crossed his face.

But when he had not returned after five minutes, I realised that he was meeting with a marked reluctance on the part of HQ personnel to hand over a uniform mackintosh for such a purpose. So I gave in, and walked the man into the building naked as he was.

We sat him in the back office out of public view, and eventually an old uniform mac was found and given to him.

A van was summoned to remove him to a Bridewell—the Merseyside term for a police station with facilities for prisoners. It came via Renshaw Street where it had picked up the streaker's clothes.

I took him out to the van, wearing the borrowed mac. We then made our way to Copperas Hill Bridewell. He was invited to put his own clothes on but refused to do so on the grounds that they were dirty.

The police mac had been lent on the strict condition that it would be returned promptly. So, as I left he was being pushed into a cell, still naked.

After completing the necessary paper work, I arrived home later than expected. I explained the delay to my better half.

'You put him in the car?' she said, obviously not very happy with the idea and entertaining doubts about the cleanliness of a certain part of his anatomy. And ever after she delighted in telling any friend to whom we gave a lift in the rear seat, who had sat there before them.

David Williams *is an Inspector in Merseyside Police. He is 42, and has 21 years' service. He is married with one daughter.*

23 Pig in a Poke

by Grace Adamson

It was my first afternoon back after three days off. Winter was advancing and there was a freshness in the air. I entered the station and headed straight for my work tray. It was I.C. week and I decided to see what delights had been placed in there during my absence. I was relieved to find nothing out of the ordinary but, there was still time, I reminded myself.

I set out for my rural patch, firearms applications and pig licences at the ready. The afternoon passed peacefully enough and I returned to the station at 5.30 pm for my meal break. Again, the cursory glance in my tray. Yes, there it was. I knew I couldn't get through an I.C. week without one, a warrant. So what?

The warrant was for John R, the younger of two brothers well known to myself and my fellow colleagues. In fact scarcely a week passed without dealing with one or the other for something. I glanced at the warrant, not backed for bail, first job after tea. Seemed best bet. John and brother Peter were strapping fellows, heavily built and capable of consuming large amounts of alcohol. They were not what you could honestly call 'clean-living'. Peter boasted of the address 'The Shed', Derby Road. The shed was situated on a pig farm not far from the A38.

Light had faded as I went to the farm. I knocked on all the shed doors but could get no reply. I could hear the pigs snorting and I jumped as a donkey nuzzled me from behind. No sign of John. I often wondered what device warned them of approaching police officers. I walked further down the field cursing that I'd left my torch in the car. Then it happened.

I stepped on to apparently firm ground and immediately sank into a soft, smelly substance. I leave a more explicit description to the imagination. I stepped out as best I could and squelched back to the car feeling disgruntled . . . and I still had the warrant for John.

I returned to the station and my colleagues held their noses in disgust. I heard someone say 'Just because you work the

WHICH ONE OF YOU PIGS DID THAT ?

rural beat there is no need to come in smelling rural.' I was not altogether amused and cleaned up as best as possible.

I got my own back. That night was the dreaded quick change over and I arrived back at work for the six o'clock start. I enlisted the help of a colleague and returned to the pig farm. I donned a pair of borrowed size 10 wellies on to my size six feet and trudged across the field, memories of the previous night still vivid in my tired fuddled brain. Smoke was puffing out of a 'chimney' of one shed so we picked our way delicately across and hammered on the door. No reply. We knew John was there and we tried all the tricks but he was wise to them, as he ought to be. After a few minutes of futile entreaty we sought other lines of attack. Just then my colleague found a piece of round flat tin and, balancing precariously on the corrugated iron window, placed it on top of the chimney. It wasn't long before a spluttering John stumbled out of his salubrious abode. His language was as ripe as the country smells. His first comment? 'You s—t pigs.' What could I say? Words for once failed me. A fortnight later John was back living in his pig sty and the fun started again.

Grace Adamson *is a WPC in Derbyshire Constabulary. She is 23, single, and has nearly five years' service.*

24 Canned Cat

by Keith Clegg

It was obvious from the outset that this was not to be one of the more memorable days of my career.

I huddled down into the panda car seat, and pulled my coat collar up higher as the early morning rain persistently poured down. It was only the incessant drumming of the hail, rain, cats and dogs upon the car bodywork, that kept me awake.

I never did care much for the early day shift, and I wished yet again that I had gone to bed early the previous night. Instead, I'd nipped out to the local hostelry for a quick nightcap and well, I did have the sense to get to bed eventually, but before that one thing led to another, you know how it is.

I glumly surveyed the rain-lashed streets outside. I had parked up on the edge of one of those 'problem family' council house estates. The cardboard and paper litter lay dank and sodden all around, too apathetic to be blown about by the blustering breeze.

I was quietly envying all these people who would be enjoying their Sunday morning lie-ins, when the unpredictable happened.

From across the road, a front door crashed open and a boy about eight years old came dashing through the rain towards me. In seconds he was soaked to the skin, and his clothes had become bedraggled rags. He was crying bitterly as he frantically pummelled the driver's window to attract my attention.

I wound it down approximately half an inch, so that none of that foul weather could contaminate me, tilted my head back, lined the boy up at the end of my nose as if I was sighting a gun at him, and inquired 'Yes?'

'Can you help me mister?' he pleaded . . . 'Please help me, me cat's got its 'ed stuck in a tin of cat food an' it can't breathe! It's suffo-kettin' an' chokin', an' I can't get the tin off its 'ed! Please 'elp me mister! Please!' he concluded, panic-stricken.

"AND MY OLD MAN SAID THERE'S NOT ENOUGH ROOM TO SWING A CAT IN HERE"
CORN FLAKES

I sighed as I hauled myself out of my cosy little panda car and stepped out to sample the delights of a typically British Sunday morning.

Somehow the boy and I struggled across the road and into the sanctuary of his home and, sure enough, in the front room, writhing and squirming on the hearth rug, with its head firmly wedged inside a slim tin of cat food, was a marinating moggy, desperately trying to eat its way out.

Mum, dad, grandma, brothers and sisters, and an odd neighbour or two, were all gathered around, staring blankly at the frantic feline. Then they looked at me and my uniform in wonderment, expecting us to do something.

I just stood there feeling wet through and miserable. My brain had switched off, and I was fresh out of miracles for the day.

Then came a flash of inspiration. If I could get a tin-opener, I could get the closed end of the can off, scrape the food out, and 'Tiddles' would be able to breathe again. A pair of tinsnips would remove the rest of the can, but first I had to get a tin-opener.

I asked the lady of the house for one, and explained what I wanted it for. Saying 'That's a good idea, why didn't I think of that?', she swept the canned cat up into her arms walked briskly towards the kitchen door, while I squelched along in her wake.

She entered the kitchen, and as I looked over her shoulder I could see, on the far wall towards which she was heading, there was one of those . . . one of those . . . wall-mounted can-openers.

'Oh, no! Not that!' I thought 'Please no! She can't do that! She mustn't!'

She did. There was a deadly clunk as she rammed the tin into place, and then the horrible rattle and squeak of metal being torn apart . . . Oh, it was horrible! Horrible!

Trouble was, she was holding the cat's hindquarters firmly and immobile in her hand, but the can, which contained the top half of the cat, was whizzing round in circles, and all one could hear were muffled feline-type curses emitting from inside the can.

However, all good stories have a happy ending. We did manage to rescue the cat, and I did manage to borrow some tinsnips from a neighbour, with which I cut 'Tiddles' free from a fate worse than wall-mounted can openers.

I got some right earache off my pals at the police station when they found out about that lot, I can tell you, and even now, years later, they still ask me to recount the events of that sad and soggy day.

And when they ask me if I managed to save the cat, I always reply, 'No, I took the cat off her in the end, and then I shot the poor thing, to put it out of its misery!'

25 The Card Players

by Jeffrey Wilkinson

Police officers are the sort of people who do not lightly say things which are likely to bring disrepute or ridicule (or more heavily than necessary) on themselves.

Having said that, it is also fair to say that there are people who have an awareness for things that are not within the bounds of normal experiences.

If one takes the area of such experiences, which are classed generally as supernatural, add to this the normal thoughts of policemen and you have the ingredients either of an interesting experience or cynical disbelief.

While I make no claims to being in communication 'with the other side', or having special powers of perception, I have an open mind on this type of matter.

I bring to mind two incidents where no logical explanation could be found. One of these took place whilst I was still in the RAF, the other when in the police.

The latter incident happened when I had about two years' service. On a period of night duty the set of beats to which I was detailed was a longish one, three and three-quarter hours each time round.

It was clear moonlit night with no mist, smoke, fog or anything else which might have given an easy explanation of what was to happen. The moon was three-quarters full, and its relative position could not have cast any shadows.

On this beat, I had unoccupied houses to check, these being on the opposite side of a large cemetery. I had a choice of either going through it, or walking round it. The shorter distance won.

Going down the main drive of the place, I had no qualms whatsoever. Passing the chapel, some 30 yards ahead was an open area. On this piece of ground was what appeared to be work-benches and seated around the benches, apparently going through the motions of eating, drinking and playing either cards or dominoes, were a number of people—about a dozen.

I rubbed my eyes, checked the position of the moon—the people were still there. Finding the nearest tap, normally used for getting water to fill the flower vases on graves, I put my head under it. Another look, they were still there.

I can't say that I was frightened, puzzled would be more accurate. Moving slowly nearer, they looked so lifelike—had I found a group of silent pranksters?

Moving in as quietly as I could, I was wondering which of the jokers I would be able to get my hands on. I was now in to them as close as 10 yards. They were still there and it was almost like watching a silent film.

Getting ready for any move, I wasn't really ready for what did happen. The whole group, benches, pots, beakers, cards—all disappeared. There was nothing except a plot of grass.

There could be no calling up on a radio—we didn't have them in those days. And you certainly didn't make such a thing known to the rest of the relief, for obvious reasons.

Still puzzled, I made it my business to work that beat for the rest of the week, instead of some shorter beat. That alone made some of the others suggest various activities I had in mind.

The night after the 'incident' was almost identical in conditions. I made sure that I was around the cemetery at about the same time. There was nothing, not even any sign of anything having been there. (To be honest, I didn't really expect to find anything.) There was nothing to be seen the rest of the week.

Some two weeks later, I was working a day beat and was near the cemetery. The houses were still on booking, giving me a very good reason for being so far across the beat.

Seeing a team of grave diggers and a supervisor, I managed to get the leader on one side.

I pointed out the piece of grass, asking, 'What is that bit of lawn about?'

'There should be a stone there, but it is being renewed,' he said, 'it marks the site of a mass grave.'

I asked: 'What is its significance?'

He replied: 'During the war, a clothing factory was on shift work. When the workers were having their meal break on one of the upper floors, a fire started. Most of them were trapped in the fire and killed.

'The factory lay derelict until a while after the war and was then turned into a showroom.'

Pressing him further, I asked: 'What time of the day was it?'

'Well officer, I was in the army at the time, but the tale is that the fire must have been on the go at about midnight to half past twelve—the anniversary was a little over a fortnight ago. The memorial tablet was moved two days or so before, as it was found to be split.'

As I said, I have an open mind. Have you?

Jeffrey Wilkinson *is a Sergeant in the Training Department in Hampshire Police. He is 48, and has 24 years' service. He is married with three daughters and one son.*

26 The Call Out

by Kenneth Brierley

It was Friday, not too busy a day. The usual run of the mill petty thieves, burglars arrested and charged, interviewed re other offences. It is 10 pm and as duty DS on call for the night, enough was enough. Time, I thought, for those few statutory drinks before 11 pm. That would bring me the repose I desired, and not a night tossing and turning with thoughts of 'Have I done this, have I done that'. Oh, they were enjoyable all right, after all it was a warm humid night late in summer.

Is that a bell ringing? Surely not. It can't be 7.30 am already. Doesn't sound like the alarm. 'Aren't you going to answer it then?' came a sleepy voice nearby. 'Oh yes love, is it the phone?' Propping myself up I reach for the phone, at the same time, with one eye only (the other just wouldn't open) I see that it is 5 am. 'That you, sarge?' 'Sorry to disturb you, there's been a bad sexual assault, she's at the hospital.' 'No we've got no one for it yet.' 'You'll go straight there did you say?' 'OK, I'll let the night inspector know.'

Some 10 minutes later I walk in a side ward. Lying in a bed a very pale female about 35, obviously in pain despite being heavily sedated. A young policewoman is standing by the bed. The local police surgeon greets me and continues to attend to the woman. I address the PW 'Whats the score, love?' 'Well, it's sodomy, and he's, er, he's used a bottle on her, you know, her private parts. I've taken a statement, she knows him apparently.' I quickly read the statement. 'See that sergeant!' It's the police surgeon pointing to a swelling in the unfortunate woman's abdomen. 'Peritonitis that! We'll have to operate soon to save her life.'

A quick phone call brings a reliable DC from his bed. 'That you Brian? Listen, this is the score.' I quickly fill him in with the details. 'Get to so and so, and if its locked use a broad fitting timpson on the front door. I want bed sheets, pillows, towels, underwear the lot. Bag it all for forensic and listen we're looking for an empty beer bottle. Find that, whatever

" PERHAPS IT'S THAT BEER THAT CAN REACH THE PARTS THAT OTHER BEERS CAN'T REACH."
X-RAY DE
NO SMOKING
B.U.P.A

you do. I'll join you as soon as I can.' Meanwhile I was allowed to talk to the poor woman who reiterated her statement and gave me the address of the offender.

As I am about to leave the hospital a short time later I am called to the phone. 'Listen, sarge I've turned the place upside down, got all the forensic, but I can't find a bloody beer bottle anywhere.' 'OK, go back there, I'll join you.'

Dare I ask the question or would I be laughed at? 'Doctor, we can't find the bottle anywhere. I don't suppose it's still . . . ' Before I could finish a burst of laughter. 'Well I can assure you, sergeant, wherever it is it's not you know where.' Silly bloody question anyway, I thought to myself.

I joined Brian at the woman's house. Another search—nothing. Returning to the station we are informed the offender has been arrested by other officers as instructed and is on his way in. Interviewed, a frank admission follows and the 65,000 dollar question 'What did you do with the bottle?' Well, following consumption of 10 pints of the best local bitter brew, he could only remember not being able to retrieve it and leaving it in the offending site. Simultaneously the phone rings. 'It's for you, sarge. It's the hospital.' Was it possible, no it couldn't be. 'Hello, sergeant. Er, we've found the bottle. It was in the abdominal cavity. Shows clearly on the X-ray. She'll be all right when we've operated.' I'm listening but also seeing the police surgeon pointing to the so-called peritonitis.

When shown the X-ray photographs at the subsequent trial, the look of incredibility on the faces of the barristers and judge just about said it all. A right call out, that one.

Kenneth Brierley *retired from Greater Manchester Police as a Detective Sergeant after 25½ years' service. He is 54 and is married with one son aged 17.*

27 The White Shawl

by A. A. Clark

I picked up the paper to catch up on the news I had heard in snatches on the car radio. I was flicking through it when my eye was caught by a picture of a nurse holding a new-born baby, under the heading: 'Police search for mother of baby left in hospital toilet.'

It took me back 30 years to April 11, 1952, a bright Saturday morning, and I could see a very young police officer walking up the stairs of Ealing Broadway station clutching a new-born baby wrapped in one of the finest white shawls you could wish to see.

I could even remember thinking 'If I fall over or trip, goodness knows what I will do'. Everybody was stopping to stare. If it hadn't have been for the shawl I could have tucked it under my tunic and got away with it.

Then, back at the nick, just imagine the greeting I got as I climbed out of the car. There was Fearless Fred, the Station Officer. I think that for the first time in his illustrious career he was a bit taken aback, but he followed me into the front office and, placing his big chair alongside the fireplace, told me: 'Sit down, lad. I'll get the WPC.'

But just as he said it, in walked Shirley Thomas, detective sergeant. What was it, she asked? Boy or girl? I didn't even know, but a quick peep revealed a boy about 10 days old, extremely well dressed and cared for, a nappy with waterproof pants, vest, matinee coat, booties and this very long white shawl. All the clothing was of the very best quality, but every name tag had been removed.

The only WPC on duty that day was at Southall on an inquiry and would not be back until about 1.30 pm, so there we sat in front of a fire in the front office of Ealing station.

Earlier that day a woman carrying our baby had got on an express at Paddington bound for the West Country. The first scheduled stop was Exeter, but at Ealing Broadway the train was halted by a signal because of men working on the line.

For a few seconds it was alongside a platform. The woman opened the door of her carriage, walked about six paces to the waiting room, placed the baby on the table and returned to the train just as it pulled away.

Nobody could supply any information as to the identity of the woman—there had been nobody on the platform, since the express was not supposed to stop there, and nobody in the waiting room. It didn't seem possible and yet, back at Ealing nick, a young police officer sat holding a very young baby who was still sleeping peacefully.

At 1.30, I handed him over to the WPC. He was then taken to King Edward's Hospital, still asleep, and two days later transferred to a children's home. Despite extensive inquiries by the CID and uniform branch all over the country, the mother was never traced.

Fearless Fred has since died, the old Ealing nick in the high street has been demolished, King Edward's Hospital has gone too, and I've retired.

I still wonder how mothers can do it.

A. A. Clark *was a PC in the Metropolitan Police but now works for a construction company as a security officer. He is 60, served nearly 30 years in the Met, and is married with two children and three grandchildren.*

28 On the Dog Watch

by Colin Chandler

Gainsborough used to be quiet. In 1959 it was very quiet, but it was a great place for a bobby to learn his trade. On quiet days we used to do wildly exciting things like checking a whole street for dog licences. That was usually on Monday morning.

At most places the door would be opened by the lady of the house, bedraggled, wet through, and splattered with soap suds. Monday was always washday. The dialogue went something like this: 'Morning. Have you got a dog?' That was always the first question—unless a shabby mongrel had already answered it by darting ahead of his mistress to attach himself to the end of your trouser leg. Then Question One was: 'May I see your dog licence, please?'

You were then either invited to put the kettle on while the lady of the house hunted for the licence, or you were asked to do the hunting while she had a final thrash with the dollypegs. Then she put the kettle on. This was real community policing.

The sergeants who governed our lives then were obsessed with the need to see that we kept a tight hold on the dog licences. Found and stray dogs were treated with much more urgency than the odd prisoner. So it seemed perfectly natural one day when the whole divisional machine swung into violent action in the hunt for a 'lost' valuable golden labrador from the Uphill area of town.

A couple of days later, arriving after refreshments on late turn, in the rain, I was met by the unusually smiling Sergeant. 'I think we've got 'im,' he said.

'Great,' I said, looking forward to the end of observations for a regular breaker who was giving us a bad time.

'No, the labrador. He's in the kennel in the yard. Take the Land-Rover and one of the lads and take him to Cherrytree Road and let the owner have a look at 'im.'

I had really made the big time. I was just out of probation and I had been given sole command of his cherished

GET READY....
PET SHOP
RON COOPER
THE DOG AND BON
POLICE
POLICE
HALT.

Land-Rover, which was normally used only in time of haemorrhage or flood. It was one of the canvas top jobs. You got in the back by rolling up and securing the flap containing a celluloid window and dropping the hinged tailboard.

The large, wet, doleful looking labrador wasn't keen to get into the Land-Rover. No amount of 'Hups' or 'Good boys' would change his mind. He just stood there looking totally miserable. My colleague and I decided to load him ourselves.

It was now dark so the sergeant held the torch. The animal assumed an obstinate stance, which meant that whatever end you got hold of he kind of bent in half, away from the direction of travel. Eventually, sagging horribly amidships, we folded him, battened down the hatches, and were off Uphill.

I knocked at the door. The man opened it and was chewing heavily on his tea. Proudly I announced: 'I think we have your labrador, Sir. Will you come and have a look please?' He grunted, nodded and, still chewing heavily, followed me up the garden path to where my mate had opened up the back of the Land-Rover and was shining his lamp on the incredible hulk, which was lying fore and aft with its tail nearest to us. Whatever the man had in his mouth, he was still chewing it.

'Can I see his face', he mumbled. My mate and I looked at each other. He had the light, so I climbed in, and turned the animal's head and doleful eyes to the right. The man tilted his head first to one side and then the other, looking hard at the dog. He looked puzzled. The rain was pouring down.

'Can you turn him right round so I can see him head on?' he asked. My mate and I looked at each other. He had the light, so I heaved the creature round in sections until all of it was roughly in the right order and facing the man. The two gazed at each other.

He again tilted his head from side to side, and finally swallowed his tea. Taking a deep breath he said: 'No, he's not mine. Mine's in the 'ouse. Come home the day after we lost 'im.'

For a moment I lost my self-control. I was still lying alongside the now slobbering hound. I couldn't believe my ears. 'Well why the hell have you had us heaving this thing about if yours is in the house?'

'Well', he said, 'I just wanted to be sure the right one had come home. You never know, do you?' Then he was off up the path, to finish his tea.

Colin Chandler *is an Inspector in Lincolnshire Police. He is 47 and has 26 years' service. He is married with three daughters, Tracy 23, Debra, 20 and Nichola, 18.*

29 Coppering

by Paul Rowlandson

In the days before personal radios, when the only other policeman you were likely to see during the watch was the sergeant, the only source of instant advice and help was the phone. In Liverpool with no police boxes this meant the public phone and so the importance of always carrying at least four pennies in change was regularly impressed on the new recruit.

One evening I left the station with 12 coppers in my pocket and four months' service in the book. I was fully equipped to meet any emergency. The first hour was quiet and I rang my wife to reassure her, 'Don't worry, love, it's dead tonight.'

I left the phone box and walked on down the main road. As I rounded the bend half-way down I could see the headlights of a car shining along the pavement. Having convinced myself it was not moving, I approached to investigate. The car was in fact parked at right angles across the mouth of a side street completely blocking the road. I found all the lights were on, all the doors were open and the inside looked like a tip. Even my short experience told me there was a good chance it was stolen. After switching off the lights and closing the doors I walked quickly back to the phone box.

I deposited my four pence, pressed button 'A' and was through. My inquiry revealed that the vehicle was stolen and I was told to return immediately and stand by to await the towing vehicle. Feeling quite pleased with myself I returned to the car and waited.

Time passed and I was beginning to wonder where the towing vehicle was when a man came running towards me, 'Officer, officer, there's a fire!' I ran across the road and round the bend to see thick smoke coming from the basement of a clothing warehouse. The place was locked and in darkness so I ran the 200 yards to the now familiar phone box, dialled 999 and called the fire-brigade. I got back quickly to the scene where the fire seemed to be getting a hold and the inevitable crowd was beginning to gather. I kept them at a safe distance and in no time at all the fire-brigade sped round the corner, came to a stop, and rapidly tackled the blaze.

As things got organised I was approached by the fire officer who asked me for a keyholder. Realising I had forgotten to ask for one I returned again to the phone. Putting my last four coins in the slot I spoke to the keyholder and returned to the warehouse. The fire was now being damped down and I began to get details for the report.

Suddenly there was a squeal of brakes and an almighty crash. The fire officers' van was sandwiched between the fire-engine and a newly-arrived car. There was water and steam everywhere. A quick check revealed that the four occupants of the car were just shocked and shaken which described my feelings exactly. I now had an accident report, a fire report, a stolen car and a crowd to deal with. I had no money to phone as that call to my wife had used my change. I could not leave the scene, as I might wish to. Despite there never being a policeman when you want one a traffic car miraculously appeared. My youth and relief obviously showed because a reassuring voice said, 'Don't worry, lad, we'll deal with this. He jumped the lights down the road.'

Keeping one eye on the crowd I continued with my fire report but not for long. I felt a tap on my shoulder and a voice said, 'Towing truck. Where's this car then?' I walked down the road and round the bend towards the side road and the abandoned car. The closer I got the more my heart sank. The car was not there. Praying that someone had pushed it off the junction out of the way I arrived at the corner but the side street was empty.

'It was just here, but it's gone,' I said weakly. 'I can see that, lad,' came the unsympathetic reply. I began to explain that I had been dealing with the fire and then this accident happened. 'Ask for help, lad, haven't you got fourpence? Didn't you learn anything at training school?' Before I could reply they were walking away wondering aloud about the standard of new recruits and I was left thinking that if tonight was what was meant by 'coppering' I still had a long way to go.

Radios now provide instant assistance and that phone box was long ago converted to STD but I still think twice about ringing my wife from work.

Paul Rowlandson *is an Inspector in Merseyside Police. He is 36, and has 16 years' service. He is married to Pauline, and has two children, Clive aged 12 and Helen aged five.*

30 Case of Mistaken Identity

by George Wells

It was during 1963, in my first six months as a probationer in the Birmingham City Police, that I realised that as a police officer, I was going to find myself in positions where I would have difficulty preserving my dignity.

Officers attending court when not on duty were then allowed to travel to and from the court wearing civilian coats over their tunics. I had gone straight from night duty to the Victoria Law Courts in Birmingham.

As I left the court I was approached by another officer wearing a short, white raincoat the same as mine. I had seen him before in the main hall of the building. We chatted about the job as we walked through town until, when we were near my bus stop, I commented on his trousers which seemed to be made of a material slightly different from mine. He said it was all down to the Duke Street stores, which I could well believe.

Then he said he was very pleased with the modern handcuffs he had been issued. It was then I realised I had an imposter on my hands: the Birmingham City force did not issue handcuffs then.

I guided the man into a shop doorway, where he became a little shirty. I took from him the cuffs and a truncheon and told him he was coming with me to Steelhouse Lane station. People must have wondered about these two coppers who were such close friends one was holding the other's arm.

I walked into the charge office, holding my prisoner tightly by the arm and confronted the duty inspector. 'I've just arrested this man for impersonating a police officer.' The inspector stared first at my prisoner, then at me, and said; 'Well, who the bloody hell are you, son?'

I introduced myself, but he didn't seem convinced, so I took off my mac to reveal my tunic jacket. My prisoner didn't have a tunic under his mac. The inspector was satisfied.

He told me to sit in the interview room with my prisoner while he made some telephone calls. He returned some time later, called me out of the office, and told me that, by

"I MUST BE MAD. I LOCKED HIM UP WHILE I WAS OFF DUTY."
WELLS

coincidence, the force had received a letter that day from a psychiatrist who had been treating my prisoner for mental disorder. He was so concerned about the mental state of his patient, who had said he wanted to kill someone, that he had written to the chief constable.

The inspector pondered the prospect of charging the prisoner with possessing an offensive weapon and impersonating a police officer, then decided to call two doctors. The prisoner was made the subject of a detention order under the Mental Health Act.

I was looking forward to going home to bed, when the inspector told me to escort the prisoner and the mental welfare officer to the Rubery Hill mental hospital.

At the hospital, the reception clerk looked at the prisoner, then at me, and asked me: 'What's your full name and address and who is your family doctor? I said indignantly: 'He's the patient; I'm a policeman.' The clerk just shook his head and began writing.

I wished I had discarded my white mac, but it was too late and I was tired. We were ushered into a cubicle containing a bed and two seats. The patient evidently looked more of a policeman that I did, so I decided to save the doctors any confusion. As the admission doctor entered the cubicle, I immediately stood up, leaving the patient seated, staring out of the window in boredom.

Before I could speak, the doctor threw a pair of pyjamas on the bed. 'Come on lad,' he said to me, 'get that silly uniform off and get into bed. I'll be back to examine you in a minute.' He turned and left and so did I. Suddenly, I didn't feel tired any more.

George Wells *is a Detective Sergeant in West Midland Police. He is 39, with 20 years' service, and is married with two children aged 10 and 12 years.*

31 Which Way to Barmouth, Please?

by R. A. Mills

In telling this story, 20 years after the event, I am certain to destroy the faith that at least one Birmingham family has in the high standard of police training; so to them, whoever or wherever you are, I apologise.

It was 4 am on what looked to be the start of another hot August day in 1962. As I made my way down Hagley Street, Halesowen, life was beginning to stir again and with all my property checked I was able to stand a while and listen to the dawn chorus—not the sweet sound of Berkeley Square, you understand. In this area the birds tend to cough rather than sing, and the absence of the Conservative nightingale gives way to the Labour 'soot ridden' sparrow.

As I stood there in this Black Country town, alone like the first stick man on a new Lowry canvas, I was reminded of something I'd overlooked about this particular day. Today was the start of the annual fortnight's industrial holidays. This day signalled the mass exodus of nine-tenths of the population of Birmingham to the four corners of the globe. Some would be flying to Mijorker, Ibeezer and the Grand Canneries and some to Cleethorpes, Clacton and even to Rhyl.

It seemed to me, however, that most of them came through Halesowen on their way to Barmouth. Some, with little sense of direction, also came through Halesowen on their way to Scotland, London and Hull.

Many floundered in the 'Halesowen Triangle' simply because of the confusion caused by their encounter with their first forked junction since leaving Brum. Perhaps I can explain it like this: as you entered Halesowen from Birmingham the right fork was the A458 to Stourbridge, Bridgnorth, Shrewsbury, Welshpool and to Barmouth; the left was the A456 to Hagley, Kidderminster, Tenbury and not to Barmouth. It doesn't happen now—the left fork finishes at the back of Woolworth's. Luckily, the right one still goes to Wales.

In theory, once you get on this road you should not get

..THEN TURN TO PAGE 74. FOLLOW THE A31 TO THE EGG BUTTY STAIN AND TURN SHARP RIGHT TO..
THE AMAZING BOB MILLS
AA
AA
AA
ADH 7B

lost—at least not until you reach the wilds of Wales. In practice, however, the intrepid holidaymaker from Handsworth often got it wrong at this junction and got lost within 10 miles of home.

It was the car full of obviously lost people that reminded me of the importance of this particular day, and as it stopped beside me the familiar question, 'Which is the way to Barmouth, please?' rang out loudly over the noise of the birds.

Now, there are a variety of ways of giving directions to lost souls. These range from the general arm waving, turn left, straight on, turn right, etc, to the drawing of amazing diagrams on the back of Woodbine packets. There is the 'shove over and I'll take you' type, and there are those like my old sergeant, who had the unfortunate habit of adding the word 'right' at the end of every command.

His directions would sound like this: 'Go down here, right, turn left, right, then turn right, right, and left, right, OK right, cheerio, right.' I have seen some of the recipients of his handiwork coming back in the opposite direction 20 minutes later still looking for a left right right junction.

There is also the officer who starts to give directions, keeps changing his mind about the best way to go, and ends up telling the driver it would be better not to start from there in the first place, but that's another story.

As I began to explain the way to Barmouth, I noticed on the parcel shelf of the car an AA book, not the 'How to give up drinking' kind, but the 'How to avoid the most expensive garages and hotels' kind, with maps. I asked the driver to pass the book to me, found the relevant pages and pointed out how to get back on the A458. I also showed him the route of the road to Wales.

While doing this, and for some inexplicable reason, I mentally noted the page numbers and the grid references of his journey. The grateful motorist drove off in his quest for the sea. He didn't return, so I presume he found it. Meanwhile, I continued my wanderings.

Ten minutes later a battered Ford Anglia spluttered to a halt opposite me. It was loaded with kids, grannies, buckets, spades, suitcases and tents.

'Which is the way to Barmouth, please?' came the anticipated question from the Brummie 'Blashford-Snell'.

I walked over to them. 'Have you got an AA book by any chance?' I asked.

'Yes,' he said as he rummaged among his survival equipment in the back seat and found the key to his troubles.

'Now, sir, turn to page 24, square SO 98 at the bottom.'

'Yeh, I gorrit.'

'Now follow the A458 through SO 97, then turn to page 23, square SO 60, up to SJ 13 on the same page and then to SH 18 on page 22.'

As I was saying this the incredulous driver was following the route with his finger. When his digit got to Barmouth he said, 'Bloody hell, I dae 'now yow blokes lairned the AA bok by 'art, it's amazin'.

I couldn't resist a Dixon-type salute as I replied: 'It's all part of the training, sir, have a good holiday.' And off they went to the sea.

Bob Mills *is an Inspector in West Mercia Constabulary. He is 41 and has 22 years' service. He is married to Ann, and has a son, Russell, 14, and a daughter, Juliet, 17.*

32 Day One on Duty

by George Rafter

It was my first day of duty. Mint fresh from the training school was I. Parade at 9 am, the sergeant had said.

At 8.30 am, resplendent in uniform—even the closed neck tunic was not uncomfortable—I strode up the street. Mind you, I sweated a lot getting from my lodgings to the nick even though they were only 400 yds from the station. Keeping as close to the buildings as possible I managed the refuge of the station without being asked the way to some place, or seeing an offence.

About 9.30 am I was noticed by the sergeant. 'Read these, lad,' he said, laying a two-foot-high column of books on the table. Still on the same intake of breath he said, 'Have your meal at 1 pm and report back at 1.30 pm sharp for beat duty.'

At 1.25 pm I stood before the sergeant, booted and spurred so to speak, ready and willing to implement all that my instructors had taught me. I was told, 'You will be with Constable Jones from 2 to 4.30 pm. Be back here at 4.35 pm.'

Constable Jones was a comfortably built man, quite old I thought, about 40 he looked. 'Come on, lad,' he said, and we set off into the afternoon sunshine.

'Lad' seemed to be an expression to those without names—not an endearing term, just a word, but well understood by all, as I later found out. We walked for hours and miles and my cape felt like a large wooden cross. Finally, 4.35 pm arrived, I was back in the station.

Gratefully, wearily, but with a warm glow of day one being nearly over, I relaxed and thought the job's all right. The next half hour proved horrific.

In the charge room sat the sergeant and I. He was writing busily. Then his telephone rang. I heard him say 'I've got no one to send'. Then he said, 'Yes, all right then,' and banged the telephone down.

I then became aware that we were the only two persons in the station on duty. I also knew at that moment that something was going to happen to me, because the sergeant eyed me very thoughtfully. A bit like a small dog with a big bone—doubtfully, even. There was no escape, I was available.

'Well, lad,' he said, 'the position is like this. There is an accident just up the road, not much in it I believe. Now if I go, you have to look after the station and you cannot do that. You go and I will send a traffic car if I can raise one on the wireless.'

Armed with a street map, I set off to find the scene of this accident. My first day of duty and nearly my last.

After some 20 minutes of walking, a traffic car did pull up, and the driver did say 'Get in, lad'. He also said that he was not very familiar with the location given and he pulled up near a man who was walking towards us. 'Ask him if he knows of any accident,' said my driver.

Here was a chance to show my stuff, the high value training in action. Confronting the man I asked if he knew of the location we sought or had he heard of an accident.

'Well,' he said, 'I don't know about any accident, but if you go into that house there (pointing to a nearby cottage) a chap's just gassed himself.'

Sprinting back to the car I relayed this extra information to the driver. 'Just nip in, lad, and have a look at him and come back.'

Following in the footsteps of an old lady who was weeping copiously, I went into the kitchen of the tiny house. I saw an old, greasy-topped gas stove and, in a chair at the side with a blanket over his head, was an old man.

He was about 80, very red in the face and he looked to me to be dead. I felt his skin. It was cold and he was very stiff.

Pausing long enough to establish that he lived in the house, I dashed out and told the driver. 'All right, lad. I'll radio for an ambulance and doctor to attend', and this he did.

Giving him directions to our accident location, we went along a farm track at the edge of a housing estate. There we saw a large stationary lorry and, standing by its side, was a very white-faced man later found to be the driver.

By the side of the rear wheels was a large blanket covering a small object. We pulled the blanket aside and saw the body of a small boy whose head was crushed under the rear twin wheels of the vehicle.

At this particular point I forgot all about my training and what to do. My driver became the very experienced officer that he was and took charge. I was delegated to a distance away to keep at bay the inevitable onlookers.

As I say, it was my first day in the job, very nearly my last one. But I can say that on this day I got some service in.

George Rafter, *57, retired from Hertfordshire Police as an Inspector after 30 years' service. He is married to a teacher and has a son studying to be a solicitor.*

33 Follow That Car!

by Allan Gilbert

I was enjoying a pint with a colleague one evening in a Llangollen pub when Leon, a notorious Wrexham criminal, came in, accompanied by an incredibly beautiful girl.

Leon was as likeable a rogue as you could wish to meet: he had the looks and physique of a film star and was extremely good company. His weakness was the motor car. (He had committed every conceivable illegal act in connection with the car. His resulting disqualification stretched into the 21st century.)

As soon as he came in he spotted me. 'Hello, Allan. This is Marie. She's French.'

'Nice to meet you Marie,' I answered.

He leaned forward and whispered: 'I'll not be causing you any bother tonight, Allan.' He winked and removed his gorgeous companion to a more secluded corner.

At the end of the evening Leon and the girl left just in front of us and, although we were not watching him, we couldn't help noticing that he was heading for a car at the opposite end of the car park.

He politely ushered his companion into the passenger seat and, without so much as a backward glance, got in and drove off.

'Did you see what I saw?' I asked my friend.

'He must know we've seen him,' he said. 'Unless he's stoned.'

'Let's get after him,' I cried.

We piled into my old Beetle. Not that we needed to hurry, there was Leon, only a short distance ahead, driving rather slowly.

'Maybe he's got his licence back somehow,' my friend suggested.

'No chance—although it's just possible that he didn't see us in the car park. He's infatuated with that girl.'

My friend thought for a few seconds. 'No. I'm convinced he saw us, Allan.'

Leon was about two yards in front of me by now. I was convinced he was watching me in his mirror, but he was driving perfectly. He was even giving hand signals.

'Perhaps he's had a driving course,' said my friend.

A couple of miles on we saw a phone box. 'There's a kiosk,' my friend yelled. 'I'll get on the Ops room to set up a road block.'

I screeched to a halt. Within minutes my colleague was back and the chase resumed.

'They're setting up a road block at Wrexham,' he panted.

We caught up with Leon in the next village, still driving like a saint. Although there were a few cars between us, we could still see him clearly.

'He's giving more hand signals than a nun on her driving test.' My thoughts were interrupted by a traffic car hurtling past us in the opposite direction, lights flashing, siren blaring. But Leon, unabashed, continued calmly towards home.

Within minutes we caught sight of the road block in the distance, three traffic cars in line across the road.

'This is it Allan. He'll be away across the fields like a whippet,' my friend said excitedly.

The leading car stopped at the road block with Leon's close behind. I could see him through the rear window of his car and had to admire his nerve as he produced a perfect hand signal to indicate he was stopping.

A traffic officer ran forward to make the arrest. I saw him open the driver's door . . . and then make his way down the line of stationary vehicles. I wound down my window, but before I could speak, he hissed: 'Gilbert, you're a pillock.'

'But we've followed him all the way from Llangollen. We've got him bang to rights.'

The traffic man looked at me with a pained expression. 'It's a left-hand drive, you . . . .ing idiot. It's some foreign bird driving.'

For months later, cartoons appeared all over the nick depicting my acute embarrassment in every conceivable way.

A couple of weeks after the incident I bumped into Leon at a local night club. 'If you're worried about drinking and driving, Allan, I know of a good chauffeur,' he said. 'Funny word 'chauffeur', isn't it? It's French, you know.'

Allan Gilbert *is an Inspector in Derbyshire Constabulary. He is 38 and has 17 years' service including 13 years in North Wales Police. He is married with a son and a daughter, aged 11 and nine.*

34 Always Carry a Banana

by Terence Leathley

I haven't been able to tell this story before, just in case the principal character, the monkey, was still alive. I hate causing embarrassment.

I was policing a large seaport at the time (with a few others) and was pounding the not-very-exciting Thirteen beat. Two monkeys had escaped from the circus and were in danger of starving to death on the city roofs. A decision was taken to shoot them on sight rather than let them suffer and one of them had already bitten the dust.

It was about this time that '353' invented the 'roof game'. (We didn't have names in those days.) In full uniform and broad daylight he used to stand at the pavement edge staring up at a roof. Within a couple of minutes 50 and 60 honest citizens were doing the same thing. 353 waited his opportunity, then took his helmet off and snook away. (That used to be the past tense of the verb 'to sneak' where I did my policing.) There wasn't much else to do in those days.

When I made one of my hourly telephone calls I was told to get my body over to Spring Bank West. A large crowd was blocking the Queen's Highway and, oh yes, they were all staring up at a roof-top.

I sprinted along at the regulation two miles per hour. The theory was that if you kept to that speed the trouble was nearly always over by the time you got there. (I go into hysterics these days watching you fellows belting along with two-tone horns and flashing lights.)

When I finally did arrive there were two or three hundred people halfway across the road all staring up at the roof of a house and 353 was nowhere in sight. On the roof was a monkey. The people wouldn't shift. Not for me, anyway. I rang my friendly sergeant and asked for reinforcements.

There were no reinforcements, I was told. Everybody in the division (except me) was really busy. I had to go it alone. I explained if the fire brigade could come along with a ladder, I would apprehend the monkey and the crowd would go away.

WOULD YOU LIKE A BANANA FOR THE MONKEY?
NO THANKS

My sergeant was not at all pleased with this idea. I could tell that because it was all of 10 seconds before he gave me an answer. When it did come it was to the point: 'You are not going on no roofs. Now, get that crowd shifted.' Note the double negative. Grammar was my sergeant's only weakness and I feel sure that this saved me from a 'disciplinary'.

I immediately began looking round for a ladder. You have to have one to get on to a roof. However, at the prospect of seeing a copper tip-toeing along the roof-tops, everybody became most helpful and a ladder was soon produced. I can still hear the cheers of the admiring throng as I reached the summit.

The monkey was really startled by the face-to-face confrontation, and so was I. Having been brought up in a city, animals were not my strong point.

The monkey scurried away along the top of the roof with its arms outstretched for balance and moved very quickly. I am a quick learner and did the same. (You fellows should bear this in mind. The arms should be outstretched with the hands dropped at the wrist. But you probably call for a helicopter these days.)

I caught that monkey. Maybe its morale was low; maybe it recognised a (slightly) superior animal when it saw one, I don't know. But of all the things I did during my 30 years' service, catching that monkey was . . . but I digress.

I brought the monkey down and everyone applauded. The monkey became quite fond of me and put its arms around my neck. A kindly housewife invited us in to sit on her staircase and I telephoned for the RSPCA. While we were waiting I sat on the staircase with the monkey on my knee. A fruiterer brought us (the monkey and me) a bunch of bananas. We were enjoying them when the front door opened and there was my sergeant.

He was sweating profusely and gasping for breath, being very red of face. He had just sprinted two miles flat out on his bike to catch me on the roof-tops. He knew I would go up there. He had his faults, as I have said, but he did know the opposition.

Funny thing was, he was so pleased with himself for being right that I got away with it rather lightly.

If there's a point to the story, it's this: that sergeant used to give me a pretty rough time and I nearly packed in the job. When I went back to the nick, having been promoted a couple of times, I did what the rest of you would have done: I took a look at the records.

That sergeant had been giving me some pretty decent write-ups as a probationer. I thought some of you youngsters might like to know that. Don't despair. Most sergeants have a bark much worse than their bite.

Incidentally, I did always carry a banana after that.

Terence Leathley, *54, retired as a Chief Superintendent from Cumbria Constabulary after 30 years' police service. He is now a Security Advisor with NE Gas. He is married with a 25-year-old son.*

35 Miracles Never Cease

by John Pilkington

To make the claim that it was easier for a camel to pass through the eye of a needle than for one to receive a new piece of equipment from the supplies section of my force would not be an understatement. Nevertheless, I eventually obtained a new raincoat from them after umpteen reports requesting that I be supplied with one.

Proudly wearing the new coat for the first time, I started a night shift patrol, being extremely careful not to get the garment wet on its first tour of duty, despite a rather heavy rainfall.

After about three hours into the tour I was directed to the local Roman Catholic church to attend a report from the parish priest that a man, who was clad simply in his underpants, had broken into the church and was drinking the altar wine.

'Not too unusual an event for a town known as Scotland's largest open-air asylum,' I thought to myself and made my way to the locus.

On arrival at the church a few minutes later, the wine drinker's family doctor approached my vehicle and advised me that his patient was mentally disturbed and, should he see a police uniform, was likely to become extremely violent.

The doctor stated that he intended to have his patient admitted to a nearby mental hospital for treatment and that an ambulance with male nurses was en route. To avoid possible violence he requested that my colleague and I stand by and take no police action.

This was a request which I was glad to comply with for two reasons: (i) I'm getting too old to get involved in fights; and (ii) I still wished to avoid getting my new coat wet.

However, I did report the situation back to my control and they despatched another police vehicle, containing a male and female officer, to the scene.

A few minutes later the ambulance arrived containing four male nurses. As the doctor explained the situation to the

"RIGHT JIMMY, WE'LL TOSS UP FOR WHO GETS HIM. HEADS WE WIN, TAILS YOU LOSE."
NEW

nurses, I was confident that the police would not need to become involved in any struggle as all the nurses looked as if they were contestants for the Mr Universe contest.

However, at this moment our wine-drinking friend, still wearing only his underpants, emerged from the church. On seeing our friend, who was about twice the size of any other person, the male nurses politely declined to take any action until he was put in the ambulance by the police.

At this point the doctor returned to my colleague and I, and asked if we could persuade his patient to enter the ambulance.

'Okay,' I said, 'I suppose the coat has to get wet sometime.' So we alighted from our vehicle and approached our friend, who was at this time reciting the three times table.

Before we could use our years of experience and police charm our friend pounced on my colleague, caught him around the throat and started to strangle him. On seeing this I carried out a rugby tackle, which would have been acclaimed by anyone of Scotland's Rugby XV.

As a result, both of us fell to the ground and I landed in a pool of mud, new coat and all.

In the ensuing struggle my newly-arrived young female colleague ran forward and handcuffed our friend's left hand. She then caught hold of another hand, believing it to be his right hand, and as she was about to handcuff it we all heard screams of terror from the doctor who was extremely reluctant to be handcuffed to his patient.

Nevertheless, despite this slight setback, our friend was handcuffed and the male nurses emerged from the relative safety of the ambulance.

One of them, who was armed with a hypodermic syringe, began to gather momentum as he raced towards the patient, somewhat reminiscent of a Zulu warrior carrying an assagai.

Unfortunately, as he neared the patient he tripped on the kerb, fell forwards, and stuck his syringe into the hand of one of his colleagues.

Fortunately, the drug was not injected into the nurse and command of the situation was quickly regained, resulting in the sedation of our friend.

After this I managed to regain my feet and, as I looked

down at my mud-stained coat, a number of four-lettered Anglo-Saxon words were emitted from my mouth.

As I continued muttering these words I walked towards a small man wearing a clerical collar. Realising that it was the parish priest I immediately apologised.

In return, the priest raised his hand in blessing and said 'It's all right my son, I've heard bloody worse tonight from that daft bugger.'

His blessing must have worked miracles, as I was within days re-supplied with another new raincoat to replace my mud-stained garment.

John Pilkington *is a Sergeant in Strathclyde Police. He is 36, has 17 years' service and is married with two daughters aged nine and six.*

36 Blood, Sweat and Prayers

by John Walker

For some reason, my new-fangled radio had packed its bags and I was on my own.

I was in Abberley Street, in the rusty, dusty, ragged end of Birmingham, known as Winson Green. It was pitch black and for 10 minutes I had been struggling with 12 stones of blood-streaked, gin-soaked, blubbery womanhood, who was refusing to get into an ambulance.

My gloves had soaked up just about their limit of the woman's blood and my fingers kept slipping off her thick arms. It was like trying to knead a jelly.

I could smell that blood, even taste the odd stray spottle. I could smell the gin in her breath, and the cheap perfume that fought a losing battle with the odour of stale sweat on her skin. I was ready to walk away and leave her to her smelly, sweaty, bloody self.

I couldn't do that though. Preservation of life. First on the list of a copper's prime duties.

Even if the stupid woman had thrown herself through a window.

Even if the stupid woman really did want to die. I didn't believe that, however. If you wanted to kill yourself that way, you didn't choose a ground floor window and you opened the damned thing first.

Time was running out though. The woman had a good chance of stepping into the next world, and a lot easier than she obviously intended to step into the ambulance.

She was standing, feet astride, in her gateway, hands resting on the posts. And every time that I tried to grab her wrists, in an effort to staunch the bleeding, she would throw her arms about, spraying her life-blood everywhere.

The ambulancemen must have thought I could manage because they had merely opened the rear doors of their vehicle and with a casual 'Bring her over here then, officer', had gone to lean on the bonnet of my panda. Perhaps they hadn't noticed how much blood was raining about.

"I WANT TO MEET MY MAKER"
I'LL TAKE HER BACK TO LEYLAND TRUCKS

The woman flung her arms wide again. 'I don't want to go to hospital,' she screamed, 'I can't.' Her voice battered about the street, bringing more rubber-necks to join the small crowd around us.

Comments were starting to drift about.

'He shouldn't be 'andling her like that.'

'Got no right to make 'er go.'

And from some idiot who had missed the point, 'Somebody oughter help 'er.'

Encouraged by this, the woman screamed out again 'You can't make me go.'

Sighing, I stepped back a pace and the woman, realising that there was no one holding her now, stepped contrarily on to the pavement. There she dropped to her knees, entreating to anyone who cared to listen, 'Please don't let them take me.'

I wasn't beaten yet though. Besides, the ambulancemen had stepped over at last. I leaned over the woman and, with an ambulanceman holding each arm, stemming the flow, I tried gentle persuasion.

'Come on love,' I said quietly. 'You'll have to go to hospital. You'll bleed to death if you stop here.'

She sniffed deeply. 'I want to die. I ain't got nothing to live for.'

Having seen the inside of the hovel she called home, I felt inclined to agree with her. There wasn't a great deal to stay around for, unless you included the job of cleaning the place up.

But I had to keep trying. 'Now that's no way to talk. Let's jack this nonsense in and get into the ambulance.'

'Ain't right,' some fool commented then.

Another voice agreed, 'Ought to leave 'er be.'

I ignored it all, but the woman didn't. She looked up at me, 'I'm a Jehovah's Witness. You can't make me go'.

That was about all I needed. I leaned towards her dirty ear, 'I don't care if you're Doctor Crippen's witness,' I said fiercely. 'You're going to hospital.'

Someone with good ears said loudly, 'Now he's takin' the mickey out of 'er.'

'Should I fetch a parson d'you think?' a saintly person from the rear chipped in.

'Arr!' a stout woman from the front agreed. 'If it's religion, he can't make 'er go.'

The woman on the pavement started a dramatic bowing routine the ambulancemen moving with her. 'I want to meet my Maker,' she wailed, 'I want to meet my Maker.'

Looking at the drunken woman, I wondered. Did she want to complain? To *Him*? The Lord had never given anyone any guarantees, and even if He had, the woman would have invalidated hers years ago due to self neglect.

Again I sighed. It was going to be difficult to get her off her knees. One of the ambulancemen must have read my thoughts as he grinned at me. 'She weighs a ton I'll bet.'

'Maybe,' I agreed. 'But then I'm not a bookie, mate.'

I knew I was being uncharitable, but my patience was just about gone. I was, suddenly, no longer interested. Wasn't it the ambulancemen's problem anyway?

I was sick of the whole affair. Sick of the smell of blood and sweat, and sick of the close hostility of these idiotic people. I almost turned away there and then.

That was when I remembered something that had once been said to me. To be a policeman you have to care about people. Well maybe it was true. Maybe I did care. Even about this half-crazed, drunken barrel of lard. Maybe there was something in her worth bothering about. I would have to be cruel to be kind then.

I shrugged my shoulders, and grabbed hold of as much of the woman's hair as I could. Then I pulled. Hard! Bloody hard! It worked. She got to her dirty feet without a sound.

'Oooo, look!' some woman in the crowd said. 'Police brutality that's what it is.'

'I'm going to complain about him,' someone else added.

'Shall I fetch the parson now?' the saintly one said again.

Contemptuously I looked at them all. 'I hope this silly bugger is around tomorrow so you can give her my number.'

I pulled again on the woman's hair and this time she yelled, 'All right! I'll go, I'll go!' Then she promptly keeled over in a faint and had no more say in the matter.

I heard someone mutter, 'There's no need for a parson. She's going.' He didn't clarify exactly what he meant by *going* but he was too late anyway. I had noticed a shadowy form making for the vicarage at the end of the road.

Thankfully it was all over. The ambulance doors were closed on the woman. All I had to do now was follow them and clear up the paperwork.

I half-noticed that the ambulancemen had left the rear step sticking out, but as I didn't see that it really mattered, I climbed wearily into my panda, parked behind the ambulance.

Starting my engine I paused for a few moments, just sitting there. I had never met the woman before and I certainly didn't want to see her again. But I had tried. If she didn't make it, it wouldn't be my fault. Selfish, I knew, but satisfactory.

37 Houdini's Great Escape

by Mike Jasper

After 16 gruelling weeks at training school, I was posted to a south London division and incarcerated in Nightingale Lane Section House.

Nightingale had quite a liberal regimen and most officers there gave their rooms that personal touch by adding posters, furniture and stereos. I had a goldfish. At least that's how it started. By the time I had been in the section house a year I was sharing with several goldfish, a pair of piranhas, two frogs, a few lizards and the pride of my collection, a 3 ft long reticulate python. Although he was the pride he certainly was not my joy, as he had the meanest temperament I have ever known in a snake. His hate for mankind was exceeded only by his hate and loathing of mousekind, a species he devoured in huge quantities.

I kept several mice, but they were not permanent boarders. Friendships never really blossomed, for before I could properly get to know them the python would need feeding and I would have to despatch one or two. The python, a master of escapology, acquired the name Houdini.

His first and most dramatic escape had me hunting for two days before I decided to inform the rest of the PCs on my floor, impressing on them the need to keep it quiet. Unfortunately, most of them knew Houdini's man-hating ways only too well and, for three days, panic ensued. PCs and sergeants living at Nightingale took to searching their blankets before going to bed and sleeping with a truncheon under their pillows.

Houdini's size and demeanour were exaggerated by all—even by those who had never seen him.

'I hear he's 20 ft long and eats 10 cats a day.'

'I've seen Mike walking him down the High Street in the early hours, hoping to catch a sleeping tramp to feed him.'

'It's 60 ft long at least. Had the bloke from the Guinness Book of Records down the other day.'

PCs would shake out their boots and, as for the cleaners,

OOOH MIKE
BE SAFE AT NIGHT SLEEP WITH A COP
CANADA
SUE
WENDY
THE ANIMALS
BEA
MONKEES
TO LET OR WILL SHARE
THIS MACHINE KILLS

they went everywhere in groups—except to the fourth floor—where the dust got thicker by the day.

I could have lived with all that. But Houdini's escape had more horrendous results. It brought an enforced celibacy to the section house. Few girlfriends would come anywhere near the place.

Houdini's capture was brought about by my own attempts at a sexual conquest. I had taken a nurse up to view my record collection and we were lying on the bed listening to music. Unknown to either of us, a mouse had escaped from his cage and was making his way towards the bed. The nurse was the first to see it. Hearing a scream that would surely have registered plus ten on the Richter Scale, I assumed Houdini must have returned. I leapt up and switched on the light, to see a white mouse sitting on the bed cleaning himself.

'It's only a mouse,' I said, unable to hide my disappointment.

'Only a mouse,' she screamed. She suggested, through a veil of tears, that we go to the pub so she could calm her shattered nerves.

As we left, I opened my bottom drawer and took out a handkerchief to wipe her tears. Minutes later we were sitting in the local. With a flourish, I took out the handkerchief. She put it to her face, but suddenly turned up her nose.

'What's that smell?' And what's that stain?' she threw down the handkerchief in disgust. I picked it up and examined it.

'Snake crap!' I yelled, leaping up from the table and knocking over several glasses in the process. The bar was silenced. I dashed back to the section house, leaving the nurse sitting there.

Back in my room I pulled the bottom drawer. Underneath, in a small recess, coiled up and looking very smug, was Houdini. To show his disapproval at being disturbed, he bit me.

I didn't see that nurse again. As for Houdini, he stayed another six months and then I sold him. He did escape again, but that's another story . . .

Mike Jasper *left the Metropolitan Police as a PC after five years' service. He is now the Regional Security Manager at Heron Homes. He is 28 and married to Josephine—he has two dogs, two cats, ferrets, rats, gerbils, mice and cavies but no snakes!*

38 Waiting for Mr Johnson

by Frederick Bentley

I wonder what Sgt Trunky would have said if he had known that I had given that young girl a lift home on the back of my push-bike. Perhaps the background to it would be regarded as extenuating circumstances?

She had come off the last train at Upminster Bridge and it was rather late. She was too scared to walk home alone.

For the first time, I realised just how terrified of Mr Johnson the women on our manor were. I had to use my initiative—I had a point at 11.30. Giving that girl a lift home on the back of my bike seemed the only answer.

Of course, her fear was understandable if the description we had been given of Mr Johnson was anything to go by. It suggested that he was a sort of cross between 'Charley Peace' and the 'Missing Link'.

It was his M.O. which was so extraordinary and which made many of us believe that he was loco. He only operated from the railway embankment and attacked only those houses which had gardens backing on to the embankment.

The two cases reported from down the hill at Hornchurch seemed to confirm that Mr Johnson was not quite the ticket.

He had broken into one house while the family were asleep upstairs. The owner was a light sleeper and was disturbed by an unusual sound in the small hours. He got up, went downstairs. Everything appeared in order so he went back to bed.

The next morning there was some confusion in that household. None of the family—including the children—could find their shoes. Their small son found the solution. He called his father from the garden at the back of the house. The missing shoes were lined up in neat rows on the lawn.

They had been in their individual owners' bedrooms the night before. Nothing else had been removed from the premises. It was Mr Johnson.

The young couple a little further up the hill lived a real nightmare. They had one child, a little girl aged four. That evening her mother put her to bed and assured her that 'Daddy will come and tuck you in and kiss you good-night.' And that is what happened.

They were both in the sitting-room on the ground floor listening to a radio programme when the screams of their baby daughter interrupted the programme. Mrs X gave her husband the sort of look which, in effect, conveyed 'I've had her all day, now it's your turn'. Being a dutiful husband, he accepted that.

On entering the bedroom he saw the child sitting up in bed, tears streaming down her cheeks and her little hand pointing towards the window. 'A horrid man was looking at me, Daddy!'

Daddy smiled tolerantly. Very quietly and confidently he explained how little girls sometimes had nasty dreams and when they woke up they thought they were real. Gradually he saw his little girl's eyes close.

He tucked her up and was about to leave the room when he paused. He went to the window. It was slightly open at the bottom. He closed it and secured the catch. Before he left, he drew the curtains.

Only half an hour elapsed before there was almost a repeat performance—but not quite. The little girl's screams once again could be heard downstairs in the living room.

Daddy was becoming a little less tolerant. He went up to the child's room, and on opening the door saw that she was again sitting up and screaming. She was also pointing towards the window and screaming about 'a nasty man!'

For a moment her father must have doubted his own sanity. He could feel the draught as the cool night air wafted across the room from the open window—that self-same window he had secured such a short time before.

He went to the window and looking out he must have been almost as scared as his baby girl. A ladder was leaning against the sill of the window. He didn't own a ladder.

He did report the facts. He and his wife and kiddy slept downstairs for some time after that. We traced the ladder. Mr Johnson had borrowed it from another garden at least a hundred yards away.

The night that Fred Northover and I kept observation on

the railway embankment at Upminster: we were 'waiting for Mr Johnson'. The embankment was studded with clumps of bushes high enough to conceal a man. We did the job very conscientiously, isolated from each other.

It was a relief when the dawn came and we knew that it had been an uneventful night. At 5.45 we made our way back to the little nick in St Mary's Lane. Fred signed-off and was on his way—after all, he was a married man.

There was no early turn man that morning. As I was about to leave the telephone rang. 'Police Upminster', I identified the station.

For at least five minutes I listened to the almost hysterical utterances of the distraught man on the other end of that line. It was incredible.

Only when I saw the evidence with my own eyes did I believe it had really happened. There was a ladder, at an angle with the top of the tiles, resting on the bedroom window sill. There was the open window. But that was only part of it.

Mr Johnson had entered the bedroom, where the owner and his wife were sleeping. The lady had a penchant for chocolate and kept a bar in her handbag on the bedside table. Mr Johnson had helped himself to that chocolate. He had ignored the £2 or £3 in notes in the handbag.

The owner of the house was a city gent who wore the uniform—black jacket and vest, striped trousers, bowler hat, etc. Every night before he retired, he meticulously draped his trousers over the back of a chair in the bedroom to preserve the crease.

I still find it hard to believe, although I did see the evidence—Mr Johnson had calmly removed his own dilapidated nether garments and changed into that pair of impeccably creased striped pants.

The discarded garment was still lying on the floor at the foot of the bed when I arrived at the house.

The sequel to these events, which resembled the script from a 'Hammer Horror film', was enacted on a section of railway track in the Epping Division.

A rather weary CID officer thought the behaviour of the figure walking on the railway sleepers somewhat odd at five in the morning.

He stopped the man and questioned him about the large flat, polished wooden box he was carrying. The man was scruffy. He hadn't a clue what the box he was carrying contained.

It was a canteen of cutlery. It was Mr Johnson.

We all thought he was balmy. The court thought otherwise. That was the last we heard of Mr Johnson.

Frederick Bentley *retired as a Sergeant from the Essex County force after 12 years' service. He is 68, married and has a son still serving with Thames Valley Police. He says his is the longest serving police family—the tradition began in 1834.*

39 The Seance

by David Baggott

In the days before police computers and personal radios—it seems a long time ago now—the town where I was a probationary constable was having problems with a spate of burglaries on council estates. Five or six houses were entered every night and cash and small disposable items were being stolen.

We tried hard to catch the villains, but without success. We had plain clothes observations all night but the estates were too large and every morning the usual phone calls came in. The villains became so confident, or perhaps they were unaware, that they broke into two or three police houses.

Our shift was on nights and as it was winter we were getting fed up with observations with no results. We needed some help desperately. So desperately, in fact, that somebody suggested the supernatural. I had never been to a seance before, but if it saved me from those observations I was willing to try.

Our small mess room was prepared. The table was polished to a fine sheen. The duty officer made a set of alphabet cards and slightly larger cards with 'Yes' and 'No'. Luckily the barman had not cleaned up properly and we found a suitable glass. The witching hour had come—1.50 am as it happened.

The sergeant decided he wanted as many as possible and both meal reliefs could participate. We had night lamps in those days, not modern torches, but those with red and green filters.

With the whole shift gathered around the table and us all bathed in red and green lights from several night lamps, Mac, the seance leader was appointed by the sergeant. He had performed before apparently and so the session began.

'Fingers on the glass' we were instructed.

'Is there anybody there?' wailed Mac. No response.

'Is there anybody there?' Still no response.

'Is there anybody there?' More urgency this time.

The glass moved. I felt cold. Surely somebody is moving the glass I thought. I looked closely. I couldn't be sure. It moved slowly towards the card bearing the word 'Yes'. The

WHEN WILL I GET MY BLOODY EXPENSES?

hairs on my neck stood on end. Somebody gasped. The glass stopped and remained stationary.

'Is anybody there?' pleaded Mac again.

The glass moved straight to 'Yes'.

'Identify yourself', implored Mac.

The glass moved very slowly around the table stopping at letters on its way. Mac spelt out the letters as it went: LEE pause OSWALD (about two weeks previously Lee Harvey Oswald had been shot in Dallas, USA, following the assassination of President Kennedy).

Half the participants gasped, the other half laughed. The glass paused then started to move again. Was this another message? It moved round the table. Nobody could have been pushing it, it moved faster, round and round. It was gathering momentum as it went.

Fingers were leaving the glass until eventually it was going round the table so fast that nobody could keep their fingers on it. Finally it fell on its side and rolled to the side of the table. It was stopped before it fell to the ground by one of us who realised what was happening. He replaced it.

'We'll start again,' said the sergeant, 'Nobody must laugh, we were getting somewhere that time'

'Is anybody there?' said Mac.

'Is anybody there?' No response. 'Is there anybody there?' Still no response.

Despite many more tries there was no success.

I have often wondered if we had in fact contacted Lee Harvey Oswald and what he could have told us. Would we have been privileged to know the truth about President Kennedy or would he have been able to help us in our problem, and given us all information leading perhaps even to a commendation?

We, not our shift, did eventually manage to catch our breakers, but we had to use traditional police methods, namely plain clothes observations.

David Baggott *is a Sergeant in Thames Valley Police. He is 43 and has 18 years' service. He has four children by his first marriage, but is now living with his second wife, her two children, a dog, a rabbit and six chickens!*

40 Peelers All

by David Hadaway

The young PC, fresh from Hendon, was enjoying his first night duty with my relief, pounding the pavements of the West End of London around 5 am.

He was conscientiously shaking hands with the door handles of a small block consisting of four shops by three shops by four shops by a large restaurant in Mayfair when he heard a tapping noise coming from a betting shop. He rushed to the opposite side of the block to check the rear and found an open door. The villains were obviously using a hammer and chisel to break through the adjoining wall and reach the bookie's safe. Thank God for personal radios!

Assistance soon arrived, in the form of four equally fresh PC's, including yours truly, whose combined experience would not have earned half a long-service medal. The section sergeant was tied up and the inspector had time off so we carefully considered the problem in the true 'knowledge and reasoning' manner. There was only one answer: surround the block and send for a dog.

It seemed that the Met had run out of dogs—'Send a report to K9 department at the Yard and indent for some more,' said the relief comic—and it was left to the City of London to respond. They sent what can only be described as the result of marriage between a donkey and a wolf. Like the City's officers it was bloody enormous, and had hair like a hippie.

Anyway, the handler listened casually to our information, while doing a passable impersonation of a matador each time the other half of his team got within range. Then he opened the door with his foot, let in the animal said 'Find 'em', and shut it.

'Er. . . . is he all right on his own?' I ventured.

'Yeh, he's big enough and ugly enough to look after himself. Anyway, he ain't had his dinner yet,' said the handler. 'What's the crumpet like around here?'

After a few minutes' earnest discussion on that universal

"I DON'T UNDERSTAND IT, HE PREFERS CHINESE FOOD."
CELLINI
RESTAURANT

subject, he yawned, stretched and said: 'I suppose I'd better see where the silly old so-and-so's got to.'

Just then the door of the restaurant crashed open and two foreign gentlemen wearing long white aprons, each carrying an onion in one hand and a large knife in the other, abandoned the premises, 'Momma mia, Momma mia'. They were closely followed by the donkey/wolf.

The bold handler called unto the Lord to give him strength and then to his dog to come back. The creature returned, looking disappointed at the loss of dinner on the hoof.

Man and beast departed, leaving us to explain to the two early-morning kitchen hands—and the milkman they had met on the corner and caused to drop his crate and smash three pints of gold top—that we in general and *he*, the probationer—looking as crestfallen as the dog—had been acting in their best interests.

They did not appear convinced when we formally warned them of the possible dire consequences of leaving the rear kitchen door open. 'After all,' I said, 'anyone might get in.'

The tapping, in case you have fallen for the same noise yourself, was the tote clock ticking. Do you know, those kitchen hands didn't even offer us a cuppa after all that hanging about. There wasn't even a smile from them when the relief comic told them we had a lot in common, really. After all, we were all 'Peelers'.

David Hadaway *is a Sergeant in the Metropolitan Police. He is 36, has 16 years' service, and is married with two sons aged six and four.*

41 A Nappy Time

by Keith Thomas

So there I was, an experienced police officer, in the busy little Cheshire town of Winsford on four to midnight tour. Well, my pants weren't shiny yet but I did have six months' service, and I was in my very own blue-and-white panda car.

I was looking after the top end of town which included a couple of Liverpool overspill estates. You can always rely on the Liverpudlian to entertain the duty copper and this tour proved no exception.

Six o'clock came on my trusted Timex wristwatch when it all started.

'Control to panda seven. Panda seven are you receiving?'

Keen as mustard I drew out my plastic Pye radio.

'Panda seven receiving, sarge. I'm at Over Square, over.'

'Good. Go to such and such a number Glebe Green, report of trouble, over.'

'Panda seven received. What kind of trouble, over?'

'If I knew that I'd have told you. Now stop clucking and get on with it, over.'

'Panda seven to control, roger.'

Bloody marvellous, that, thought I. Trouble, that's all I'm told. Trouble. It could be a mad axeman chopping down all and sundry, or there again it could be a good-looking dolly bird locked out of her house.

That decided me, it's surprising the speed you can get up to in these panda cars in low gear. I'm somewhat perplexed Stirling Moss didn't have one for the race track.

Within no time at all I arrived at the given address but, alas, no dolly bird. There outside the house was an unattended county ambulance with its blue emergency lamp flashing in all its glory.

The front door was open so I just walked straight in. I did stretch my six-foot frame an extra couple of inches as my little bit of insurance for what might follow.

I can remember the scene in the living-room of that house as though it was yesterday.

NO CHANCE. I LET HER GO OUT LAST CHRISTMAS. THE BLOODY UNGRATEFUL COW.
AMBULANCE
57

There were two uniformed ambulancemen stood behind the settee.

There was a very pregnant woman sat on the settee. There were five smelly kids doing their own re-construction of World War II, and stood by the television was the husband.

His description amazed me at the time, although I've come to recognise it as fairly typical since.

He had long greasy black hair, black Pancho moustache, Woodbine in the corner of his mouth, and was dressed in dirty open-necked white shirt with matching cheap, beer-stained suit. He was drunk.

The house was such a tip that a sewer rat would have been proud of it. That's what I saw. But I'll tell you what I couldn't see—I couldn't see any trouble.

I asked the obvious question. 'What's the trouble then?'

'I'll tell you what the trouble is,' said the more alert of the two ambulancemen, 'this lady is in the process of experiencing labour pains.'

I gulped. Surely they don't want me to deliver it? My first aid training hadn't taken me that far.

'I'm sorry,' I said, 'I still can't see what the trouble is.'

'It's this lady's husband. He won't let her go to hospital,' blasted the ambulanceman.

'Is this true, you won't let your wife go to hospital to have the baby?' I croaked.

The husband glared at me and with Scouse logic said, 'Yeah that's right pal. I'm going out for a pint and she's got to stay in and look after the kids'.

As inexperienced as I was, the lady was soon on her way to hospital to do the 'business'. There was no way I was going to smack any baby's bottom.

I left then, leaving husband fuming in the role of baby-minder.

Shortly after 11 pm that same tour I got another job from control to go to the Old Star public house—complaint of a man acting suspiciously with children.

On my arrival I saw a party walking along the road away from the pub towards Glebe Green and I didn't know whether to laugh or cry.

It was the husband, the concerned father-to-be, singing

merrily in his intoxicated state as he walked homeward bound followed by his motley tribe of kids.

He's had his pint, several in fact, and his kids had been fed with crisps and lemonade as they waited outside the pub till closing time.

I'll admit to an irregularity. I didn't arrest him for being drunk in charge of his children but followed him and the kids until they were safely home.

Wrongly or rightly I decided that the 'new' mum had enough problems already. What do you think?

Keith Thomas *is a Detective Sergeant in Cheshire Constabulary. He is 32 and has 14 years' service. He is married to Joyce and has a daughter, Hayley, aged four.*

42 A Woman's Priority

by Alan Beckley

'Non-stop bus ride of chaos', screamed the banner headlines of the newspaper. It went on for a column about the incident which I had witnessed the night before. I thought—'That only tells half the story,' the most amusing bit had been left out.

It was two o'clock in the morning. I was on night duty with Ian, my usual crew-mate on the area car. So far, that night, it had been quiet.

The traffic was getting sparse and the quiet of the small hours was descending on the mid-week morning. It was October and a slight persistent drizzle made night duty rather depressing.

We decided to park the police vehicle in our favourite position on the forecourt of a garage on a main trunk road. Here we would be readily accessible to the town or country.

Ian drove to the garage and parked the police car facing, but a few feet back, from the road. The car radio and the personal radios were quiet. There was not a sound in the vicinity. I often marvelled at this: that from 7 am to 11 pm the road in front of us would be used by a never-ending stream of cars, lorries, motor bikes and pedestrians, but now not a soul spoiled the tranquillity.

We had, during the recent petrol shortage, got into the habit of parking up the police car and doing foot patrol or watching the roads for traffic offenders. At this minute, we were each waiting for the other to suggest the initiative of getting out of the car.

I heard in the distance the sound of a large vehicle approaching from my left. I remarked on it to Ian as the vehicle seemed to be moving quickly. Then I heard the sound of another, similar, engine coming from the same direction. Simultaneously, I saw a single-decker bus come round the bend on my left. It was driven far too quickly for the bend and crashed into a parked motor car on the near side of the road.

The next few seconds were acted out as if in slow motion in front of me. The first bus, after hitting the car, skidded down

"I THOUGHT YOU SAID THAT YOU HAD A BUN IN THE OVEN."
HOME SWEET HOME
CHILD BIRTH MADE EASY BY DR ST JOHN

the road, first one way and then the other. I saw the wheels lock on and off. The first bus then mounted the pavement, smashed down a road sign and ploughed on into the side of the public house on the far side of the road.

Watching this, I was mesmerised, but soon woke up when I looked back to the left and saw the second bus. It had also been going too fast, and when the driver had seen the plight of the first bus he decided to slow down, but again skidded. This time the bus had skidded to the off-side of the road and was heading straight for us . . .

'Reverse the car!' I shouted. Ian quickly put the car into reverse. By this time the second bus had mounted the kerb on our side of the road and had flattened a road sign. The front of the bus was alarmingly close. Fortunately for us, the driver brought the bus under control and stopped it several yards from where we sat.

I looked back—now the immediate danger had passed—in the direction the first bus had gone and saw a trail of devastation.

The bus had hit the public house opposite, smashing the signs off the wall and causing a huge crack next to the door marked 'Public Bar'. It had gone across the central reservation and taken with it several road signs plus some lamp standards. This bus had now disappeared from view up another road on our right. I heard the sound of an almighty crash from that direction. I jumped out of the car and sprinted in the direction of the crash. Rounding the corner I saw a scene unlike anything I had ever seen before. The back of the bus was protruding from the back of a lock-up shop. The front half was embedded in the ground floor having demolished the back room of the shop. I ran over and called out to the driver.

I pulled the emergency door of the bus open and climbed inside. The driver got out of his seat and walked down the bus towards me as if he was merely collecting fares.

'Are you all right?' I asked automatically.

'Yes,' he replied to our mutual disbelief.

I surveyed the scene. There was no roof or front to the bus. Bricks and mortar were on the seats and on the floor. The driver walked out of the accident with minor scratches. I breathed a sigh of relief as I was joined by Ian and the other driver.

I looked at the remains of the room. It appeared to have been a kitchen. There were overturned tables, cupboards and chairs, and an old-fashioned blue-mottled gas cooker lying on its side. The brick-dust formed a choking cloud. There was dead silence as we all looked at the damage.

'We'll have to tell our boss,' one of the bus drivers said practically. We came to earth with a bump.

A thought struck me. No there could not be . . . but, it was possible that people lived in the back of the shop and were now in bed above the room where the bus was now intruding.

I made my way gingerly over the fallen masonry. Inside, the shop looked strangely normal with haberdashery and ladies' garments on display. I went to the back of it and up some stairs which went above the kitchen.

I went into a bedroom. Through the brick-dust my torch made out a middle-aged couple lying in bed not 10 feet away from the bus and directly above it. I noticed that the corner of the room had been demolished. I called to them and the man woke up.

'Is it burglars?' he said in alarm.

'No, it's police,' I said reassuringly.

'It's not. It's burglars, isn't it?' he persisted.

'It's the police' I said and shone the torch on my uniform. He believed me.

'What's happened?' he asked.

'A bus crashed into your kitchen and it has knocked down the wall. You will have to get up,' I said as soothingly as possible.

'What?' he asked.

'You will have to get up. The building is not safe. The bus has smashed into the kitchen,' I pointed out painstakingly.

At this point, the woman sat up and said: 'Oh dear, I have got a pie in the oven.'

Alan Beckley *is an inspector in West Mercia Constabulary. He is 35 and has 11 years' service. He is married to Diane and has two daughters, Lucy aged 10 and Katy aged 7. The incident he describes happened while he was serving in Surrey Constabulary.*

43 Don't Trust a Clock

by Michael O'Hara

Way back in 1962, I was just through my probation in the West Riding of Yorkshire, and working 6×2D on my pedal cycle with another probationer. Collecting the mornings crop of committal warrant defaulters, each of which had to be walked or taken on a bus to be lodged, until we had enough for a van full.

One whom I intended arresting next, who we'll call Lenny Smithfield, was something of a character.—He'd done prison sentences for burglary, and was also an informant. He was not a successful thief and, recently, when the council was pressing for rent, we had a committal warrant, and his wife was thinking of leaving him, he had taken an overdose, staggered up to a constable, been taken to hospital and pumped out and saved.

When he finally appeared before the courts, the council were not going to press for rent for a while, his wife stayed, and the commitment warrant was suspended. Lenny thought this was good business all round.

Just as we were leaving the office to collect him, about 8 am, there was a 999 call from a neighbour that she had found a suicide note from him in her house.

Like many another thief before him, Lenny had not taken the opportunities allowed above, although at this time work was plentiful at local collieries etc. Now the whole circle had been completed again. So off we dashed on our three speed bikes to where he lived. Sure enough the neighbour showed us the note, and she had a key to his house, so in we went.

He'd made himself very comfortable in bed, with the coal gas pipe going under the clothes to him, although he was still clothed. At this time he still seemed warm, flexible and alive, so after a couple of squeezes to exhale most of the gas I tried the magic mouth-to-mouth, coupled with some heart massage. Soon afterwards a doctor, called by the officeman, arrived and after a shot of something directly into the heart without effect, he pronounced life extinct. He could not say how long he had been dead, because of the bed clothes, but thought about three hours.

So once again I became a coroner's officer, no need to bother with Scenes of Crime or CID, and as we carried the body out at about 9 am the sergeant rolled up on his pedal cycle, was told what had happened, said 'Save us a line Mick', and that was the sum total of my supervision on this job. Mainly through delays in getting hold of witnesses, using public transport etc, I worked 16 hours typing all this up ready for coroner and superintendent next morning.

But the highlight came that afternoon when I took a statement from the neighbour who had found the note. It seemed that after his wife left, Lenny had almost lived there, and had been left downstairs to see himself out at about midnight. The husband was a miner on day shift starting at 6 am and in order to make himself get up, used to set the large old fashioned alarm clock on the mantelpiece downstairs, so that by the time he got to it he was already up. It was behind this alarm clock that the suicide note had been left. So I asked how it was that the note was not seen until about 8 am. 'Oh,' replied the wife, 'I found it when I got up; clock didn't go off this morning and my husband slept in!'

Well, the verdict was suicide, what else could it be? But I shall always wonder just when he died and what would have happened if this clock had sounded an alarm at 4.45 am as it should have.

Michael O'Hara *is a Sergeant in South Yorkshire Police. He is 45, has 23 years' service and is married with three children.*

44 'The Little Drummer Boy' Requiem for a little girl

by Frank Fitchett

'We've got a right pair of bastards here.' This was Arthur Benfield speaking all those years ago at Hyde Police Station.

This first sentence of a briefing before my taking over the Murder Room on the once infamous and now almost forgotten Moors Murder inquiry was typically expressive of Arthur, the detective chief superintendent. A man amongst men—confirmed batchelor and wielder of a mean domino when the day's work was done.

I suppose most events described on paper either lose their impact or, conversely, can be distorted, but this one was to be different. Statements and reports there were by the thousand and the usual mass of exhibits.

But one exhibit was different—a magnetic tape. None of your modern cassettes but an old fashioned spool bearing the voice of the victim and a man and a woman.

It was discovered in a suitcase at a left luggage office.

The conversation on the tape was interrupted by the sound of recorded music, the popular Christmas version of 'The Little Drummer Boy' by the Ray Coniff Singers.

The finding of the tape had been one of the gems of detection which typified this inquiry; a left luggage label which, when the suitcase was retrieved, lifted the lid off a truly foul Pandora's Box.

Plenty has been written about the Moors Job and that tape found with the photographs, but I want to talk about what was, for us, the foulest bit of all; the background music of that winsome, gentle recording of 'The Little Drummer Boy', either to placate a frightened little Lesley Ann Downey or to drown her pleas to be set free.

Since then, regularly, 'The Little Drummer Boy' has featured every Christmas on one radio show or another, rekindling in the memory the voice of a terrified little girl.

It was realised that a radio had been switched on, rather

than a record player, and from this it was possible to prove that the recording had been made on the night that Lesley Ann had disappeared from a Christmas fairground in Manchester.

Her body was eventually found when, through the examination of photographs of the moors found in the suitcase, a search of Wessenden Head in Yorkshire got under way.

It's remarkable how the biggest jobs are often cleared up by a young bobby, as in the IRA Birmingham Bombers, the Black Panther and Yorkshire Ripper cases. Lesley Ann's shallow grave was discovered by a young recruit who left the digging area to relieve himself.

I wonder if but for that, she would ever have been found? Perhaps there was someone 'above' who gave the job a push in the right direction?

But back to the tape. Certainly John, the BBC Sound Engineer, tasked with making operational, certified copies, got to know the tune well enough. His normal job had been to use speed-up tapes to produce Pinky and Perky, a children's programme. Some change in job!

Poor John. We were all shattered but he the more so. The last time I met him, at the end of his stint, he still wasn't allowing his children out of the house. He had it all to do, did John.

The awful thing about the tape was the knowledge that the owner of the frightened little voice ended up buried on the moors, together with her fellow victim, John Kilbride.

No cause of death, but as Mr. Mars Jones (now Mr. Justice Mars Jones) said at the committal, 'children who die of natural causes don't get buried on the moors'.

They helped, those photographs of the grave areas and the recording. I suppose it was only natural for them to be taken. After all we all take recordings and photographs of the times we've been enjoying ourselves, so that we can re-live them later.

However, let me tell you this, every time the boss, Arthur Benfield, myself and the rest of the team hear 'The Little Drummer Boy' at Christmas the memories (and the tears) return.

A little voice saying: 'What are you going to do with me?'

and the harsh, peremptory tones of a man and a woman (I repeat, a woman). Wasn't there someone who once said 'Suffer little children to come unto me?'

Which brings me to the point of my little discourse. I hope that everyone who hears 'The Little Drummer Boy' each Christmas, especially Lord Longford, will take time off to remember a little girl, who would now be into womanhood and for whom Christmas is no more.

I got a BA degree in the Open University at the same time as Myra Hindley, in 1979. I don't know that I'm as proud of it as I might have been.

Frank Fitchett *retired as a Detective Chief Inspector in Greater Manchester Police after 26 years' service. He is 56, and has one daughter who is a probation officer at Stoke-on-Trent.*

45 The Christmas Card

by Anthony Paley

It was the week leading up to Christmas of 1962, a very cold winter. I was stationed at Watford in Hertfordshire and on late turn. It had been an uneventful afternoon: I was on two beat, which was located at the lower end of Watford High Street—the less fashionable end. The shops and pavements were crowded with shoppers; these were pre-traffic warden days. I was doing my best to keep myself warm and the 'No Waiting' areas free of cars, when I was 'flashed'. In those days, if one was required for a job an amber light would pulsate on the top of strategic placed pillars around the town centre.

I answered the phone and the voice said, 'Two Beat?' 'Yes' I replied. 'Man collapsed in Woolworth's; ambulance attending.' I was on the corner of Queen's Road and High Street. I looked across at Woolworth's, crowded with shoppers, nothing seemed to be amiss. I made my way into the store and saw a group of people. At their feet lay an old man, clutching a small brown bag. Immediately the small group of shoppers and assistants saw me they stood back. Everything would be OK now, the policeman had arrived, he knew what to do.

'All right stand back, give him some air, an ambulance is on its way,' I heard myself say. An old man, hands thrust deep in pockets, shopping bag over his arm looked up, and growled, cigarette stub still stuck to lips. 'He's dead mate, dead as a door nail,' and shuffled off. I felt the eyes of all those about on me and then the small knot of people started to melt away. I knelt beside the old man, one look at his face and I knew that I was dealing with my first sudden death. My heart started to sound in my ears and my brain was racing, back to the summer and Eynsham Hall.

After what seemed the customary eternity the ambulance arrived; they had bells in those days. I felt immediately re-assured. 'He's a goner, get the chair,' was the immediate diagnosis. Between the three of us—well I did carry his hat and stick—we carried him out into the ambulance. I accompanied them to the Pearce Memorial Hospital, and after a short visit to casualty, where a doctor confirmed that he was dead, we took him to the mortuary. One of the ambulancemen, with great perception said: 'This your first one?' I looked up from the body and said, 'Well yes, that is, on my own'. He smiled, 'We'll give you a hand'. We undressed the old chap and I took charge of his personal effects, which included his wallet and the small brown bag. I entered the details in the book and then made my way back along the St. Albans Road to the station.

I entered the charge room to report to the station sergeant. It was Fred Darts, a genial giant of a man who hailed from Wheathampstead and had been awarded the DCM during a Commando raid in the War. He looked up and said in his gruff voice: 'What you got there son?' I then gave my report in a mixture of formal and informal conversation that marked the relationship between constables and their supervisors in those days. 'I see,' he replied. 'Have the relatives been told yet?' 'No. I thought I'd have to look in the voters, see who lived at the address with him.' Fred looked at me knowingly, 'It's no bloody good looking in the voters lad, knock on the door, then you'll find out!'

In the meantime, the station duty officer had checked. 'Look's like just him and his wife.' I thought, perhaps a reprieve; 'I'll check with policewomen's office, perhaps one will come with me.' Fred got up from behind his desk and walked to the counter, put his large hand on the top and leaning forward he looked at me and said: 'Look son, some old lady has just lost her husband, they've probably been married for years, someone has to tell her. It won't be me, or him,' looking at the station officer, 'or any pee wee, it's going to be you, and it isn't fair on her to keep her waiting. That's the way to look at it; it might be hard to tell them but it's cruel not to.'

I made my way back towards the town. The old boy had lived in a terraced house in King Street, just at the back of Woolworth's and opposite the Robert Peel Pub. It was bitterly cold and seemed to be getting even colder. I clutched his wallet, which contained a few pounds, and the brown envelope. I had sneaked a look into the envelope. It contained a Christmas card 'To my wife' with a picture of a little old lady tending her garden with an appropriate verse inside. What should I do with it? I toyed with the idea of 'losing' it but immediately rejected the thought. Before I had time to gather my thoughts I was at the front door and knocking.

I could hear her hurried footsteps along the hall and feel my heart beating louder in my chest for the second time that day. The door opened a small stocky, homely old lady stood in the hall; she knew, there was no need for me to speak at all. 'Oh dear, oh dear, what'll I do.' I took her arm and gently lead her into the back kitchen. 'Oh my,' she sobbed. 'Oh dear.' She looked at me, soft eyes full with tears. 'He wasn't alone when he went? I couldn't bear it if he was alone.' 'No,' I lied. 'I was with him, it was in Woolworth's.' 'I knew something had happened, he was so long, did he say anything?' 'He gave me this to give you.' I passed her the brown bag containing the Christmas card.

She opened it, after a short time she looked up and said, 'You wait till I see him, I told him not to go out without a coat. I'll give him what for.' 'Yes, you do.' After a cup of tea with the old lady I made my way back to the station, a quicker step and yes, it was warmer. Late 'grub' now meant a quicker second half to the shift. I booked in for refreshments. Fred saw me, 'Everything all right then?' I looked up, 'Yes, no trouble at all skip.' Fred looked at me and smiled.

Anthony Paley *is a Sergeant in West Mercia Constabulary. He is 43, has 21 years' service and is married with three children—18-year-old Sharon, and twins of 16, Sean and Frances.*

46 On the trail of the Wee Black Beastie

by Laurence Candy

You receive a call saying that a lorry driver at the cattle market needs help. *Your* reaction might be that this is a chance to show off the art of rural policing at its best. Ours was that some idiot had locked himself out of his cab.

We got there to find our driver leaning against his vehicle, perspiring heavily. A less perceptive pair of officers than ourselves could have deduced that he had been engaged in recent physical activity. The driver, who hailed from well above the high-level heather mark, stated firmly, but with huge intakes of breath between each word, that 'One o ma beasties went o'er the side and made off doon the line'.

Further investigation revealed that the beastie in question was one of several he had been loading on to the lorry. It had jumped over the side of the loading ramp and run off down a disused railway line. He hadn't been able to catch it.

'It's jist a wee black beastie. It'll be hirpling (limping). It his a hurt leg,' the driver told us. The railway line comes to a dead end about a mile outside town on the outskirts of a village. We decided our best bet would be to get in front of the beastie. We got to the end of the line, climbed down the embankment and, having equipped ourselves with makeshift cattlemen's sticks, began walking back up the line.

We hadn't gone far when we saw the beastie, about 100 yds away and standing quite still. At that distance it was certainly black and far from huge. We approached with the patience of the hunter until, when we were about 30 yards away, the beast became aware of our presence and raised its black head, which suddenly seemed a whole lot bigger.

We made the sort of reassuring, crooning noises we hoped would encourage it to return whence it had come. It just looked at us. Stronger measures were needed. We whistled and yelled. Perhaps it took offence at the whistling. At any rate it made its displeasure abundantly clear. Ever so slowly, it lowered its head, and, dragging its injured leg, charged.

"THAT'S THE ONLY PAT ON THE BACK WE'LL GET."
CATTLE MARKET

For a split-second I couldn't move. All I could think of was that perhaps I'd been a bit hasty in turning down that suggestion from the insurance agent that I increase my life cover. My colleague was similarly transfixed. But not for long. The pair of us made off down the line like greyhounds out of a trap.

We clambered up the embankment, with the beastie close behind. At the top was a flimsy-looking wire fence. Desperate to put something between the beastie and myself, I decided on a frontal assault. I made a perfect take-off and landed on the other side face first in a newly-ploughed field.

I could see my partner scrabbling through the fence, with the beastie not far behind, clearly intent on helping him on his way. In front of us lay 100 yards of ploughed field, then safety, as the beastie, head between the wires, strained to carry on the chase. We felt safe enough at the other side to cast a quick look back and see our pursuer, with a shake of its massive head, disappear back down the line in the direction it had come from.

The lorry driver, his respiratory problems solved, arrived with several professional cattlemen and told us he thought he could handle things himself now. We told him that, despite its 'hirpling', his charge had given us a good run for our money. 'I thought the beastie micht dae that,' he said. 'But a didnae want to say—'no' after you boys were so keen to help.'

Laurence Candy *is a PC with Tayside Police. He is 27 and has seven years' service. He is married to Elizabeth, with one son, Kevin, aged three.*